A
Pocket Guide to

Islam

Patrick Sookhdeo

Isaac Publishing
and
CHRISTIAN
FOCUS

CONTENTS

Preface 5

  1 The Origins of Islam 7

  2 Islamic Beliefs and Practices 15

  3 The Quran 37

  4 The Five Pillars of Islam 67

  5 Women in Islam 79

  6 Islamic History 87

  7 Diversity in Islam 103

Glossary 113

Appendix I: A Chronology
    of Muhammad's life 125

Appendix II: Historical development
    of Islamic sects 129

Appendix III: Suras of the Quran 130

Bibliography 135

Preface

The purpose of this book is to outline the beliefs, practices and history of the religion of Islam, in order to
help Christians and other non-Muslims to understand
their Muslim friends and neighbours.

Although Islam and Christianity seem to have
certain points of doctrine in common, there is an
enormous difference between them, not only in beliefs
about salvation and Christ, but also in many other areas
affecting daily life and attitudes. This difference in
worldviews can all too easily lead to misunderstanding
between Muslims and non-Muslims. My hope is that
this book will help non-Muslims who would like to
have a good relationship with Muslim neighbours or
colleagues to be aware of some of the assumptions and
convictions that a Muslim is likely to hold. Armed with
this knowledge, the non-Muslim can avoid creating
some unnecessary stumbling blocks and difficulties
in communicating with their Muslim friends.

Within Islam there are many variations, just
as within Christianity. A short book like this must
generalise and simplify, so the reader should not
be surprised if their Muslim friend takes a different
stance on certain minor areas.

Many things are written and said about Islam in
our day. Not all of them are true. Our approach should

also be characterised by accuracy in everything. We must not misrepresent Islam or accuse Muslims of beliefs and practices that are not theirs. Furthermore, we must remember always that Muslims are people, ordinary human beings like ourselves, with the joys, sorrows, fears and anxieties that we ourselves experience. We must be filled with the compassion of Christ, compelled by His love (2 Cor. 5:14). Yet we must also be completely faithful to Christ and His teachings. We cannot alter, bend or dilute His teachings in any way.

Patrick Sookhdeo
November 2009

One

The Origins of Islam

The word 'Islam' means 'submission' i.e. submission to Allah. A Muslim is a person who has submitted. The religion arose in the Arabian Peninsula in the early seventh century, but it is said by Muslims to have been the religion of all the prophets from Adam to Muhammad.

Before the coming of Islam, Arabia was dominated by Arabic-speaking pagan tribes who worshipped numerous gods. Living amongst the pagan Arabs were communities of Jews who had settled in various trading cities, bringing with them their rabbis, Scriptures and synagogues. There were also a number of Christian communities. Pagan Arabs could thus gain some knowledge (albeit probably distorted) of Christian and Jewish beliefs.

Arabia was sandwiched between the two super-powers of the time. To the west lay the Christian Byzantine Empire, and to the east lay the Zoroastrian Persian Empire. The two empires were engaged in a long-running armed conflict with each other.

In western Arabia lay the prosperous town of Mecca, an important trading centre famous for a pagan shrine called the Kaaba. This cube-like building was the centre of a cult of sacred stones including the

'Black Stone', said to have come from heaven, which
was built into the eastern corner of the Kaaba. The
Kaaba was a centre of annual pilgrimage for tribes
throughout Arabia.

In later Muslim thought, these pre-Islamic times
were called the age of ignorance (*jahiliyya*), and were
despised as barbaric, immoral and idolatrous.

MUHAMMAD
(See also Appendix I)

His early life
The earliest accounts of Muhammad's life were written
at least 150 years after his death. All the sources are
Muslim, and there is no external (i.e. non-Muslim)
supporting evidence.

According to these sources, Muhammad was
born in Mecca in A.D. 570 or 571, a few months after
the death of his father Abdullah. His family, though
poor, belonged to the respected Quraysh tribe that
had custody of the Kaaba. His mother Aminah died
when he was six, and the little boy was then brought
up by his paternal uncle, Abu Talib, who took him on
long trading caravan trips to Syria, which was then
a Christian country.

As a young man Muhammad was employed by
Khadijah, a wealthy widow, to manage her caravan
trade. Although she was fifteen years his senior, Muhammad married Khadijah when he was twenty-five.
The marriage produced seven children (three boys and
four girls), all of whom died young, except a daughter,
Fatima, who became the wife of Ali ibn Abu Talib

(Muhammad's cousin) and mother of Hassan and Hussain. Khadijah died twenty-five years later. After her death Muhammad married a further twelve wives, thereby sanctioning polygamy.

His later life and call

By his marriage Muhammad became a person of importance and was able to find time for uninterrupted meditation on religious matters. Around the year 610, when Muhammad was about 40, he became very concerned about the irreligion of his compatriots and began to make frequent visits to a cave on the slopes of Mount Hirah, some three miles from Mecca, where he would meditate. During these periods of meditation, he seemed at times to be in a kind of trance; whilst in this condition he believed he had a vision of a heavenly being, later identified as the angel Gabriel, who gave him messages from Allah to preach to mankind. These messages were collected by his followers and eventually written down to form the Quran.

There has been much debate concerning the genuineness of Muhammad's experience in the cave and the authenticity of his 'prophethood'. For Christians he cannot be accepted as a prophet because his message contradicts Biblical teaching and because Christ was the final revelation of God to humankind.

The first Muslims

Muhammad's first followers were mainly members of his own family. They included his wife Khadijah, his son-in-law and cousin Ali ibn Abu Talib, and Zaid, an adopted son who had formerly been his slave,

a gift to Muhammad from Khadijah. The first adult
outside the family to make profession of Islam was
Abu Bakr, a wealthy merchant, who was a significant
early convert.

MUHAMMAD'S FLIGHT TO MEDINA
AND THE DEVELOPMENT OF HIS TEACHING

Most of the inhabitants of Mecca rejected Muhammad's teaching about the one true Allah. Some
believed him to be demon-possessed. The hostility
developed into violent persecution of Muhammad and
his small group of followers. Nevertheless there was
a continuous trickle of conversions to Islam, and the
number of Muslims rose to approximately fifty during
the period 610–613.

In the face of opposition, Muhammad decided to
leave Mecca. He first sent a number of his followers
to seek asylum in the Christian kingdom of Abyssinia
(Ethiopia), but he himself settled at Yathrib, a city 250
miles north of Mecca, which is now called Medina
[literally 'city', i.e. the Prophet's city]. The people of
Medina were favourably disposed towards Muhammad and his message. Indeed a group of Medinans
who had already met him and accepted his claims
invited him to their city and prepared the rest of its
inhabitants in advance for his arrival. The citizens of
Medina, wearied by years of internal conflict, were
keen to have a strong leader who might unite them.
Furthermore, Jews and Christians were at this time
sympathetic to Muhammad's teaching because of its
emphasis on the unity of God and its condemnation
of pagan idolatry.

Muhammad's move from Mecca to Medina took place in the year 622. This flight or *hijra* (migration) was the turning point of Muhammad's career, and was later chosen as the beginning of the Muslim calendar (see p. 28). In 624 Muhammad's forces gained a decisive victory over the Quraysh at the Battle of Badr, his first open battle. Muhammad's policy of sharing the booty with his troops encouraged tribes to fight on his side and swung the military balance in his favour. After Badr, war on religious grounds was sanctioned, first for defence only, but then for attack too. Eventually jihad became not only acceptable but a religious duty for Muslims.

At first Muhammad recognised the validity of the Jewish and Christian faiths, being content to preach as the prophet to his own people. Jerusalem was chosen as the direction that a Muslim should face when praying, and he adopted several Jewish practices. However friction developed when the Jewish tribes failed to recognise him as a true prophet or to practise the customs of Islam. Troubled by this, Muhammad began to assert the absolute character of the revelation that had been given to him, and claimed that it was a renewal of the religion that Abraham had professed. In this way he gave up any attempt to reconcile Islam with Judaism. The Muslim community were now commanded to face the Kaaba at Mecca when praying, not Jerusalem as previously.

During Muhammad's time in Medina, his doctrine took shape. Not only the direction of prayer, but also other areas of his early teaching were modified. At Medina, he began to teach that the Quran was the final and superior revelation. The daily times of prayer with preliminary washings now became obligatory. Friday was appointed the day for corporate worship at the mosque. The annual month of fasting was established.

In Medina Muhammad became ruler, legislator, supreme judge and military commander. As his power and influence increased so did large-scale warfare. In the ten years following the *hijra*, Muslim armies succeeded in conquering the whole of Arabia and stamping on it the religion of Islam. Muhammad was the first person to unify the Arabs as one people. He died in 632 at the age of about 62.

HADITH AND *SUNNA*

Muhammad's life-story is recorded in a number of traditions (*hadith*, plural *ahadith*), which have become a very important source of Islam, second only to the Quran itself. It is the example of Muhammad and his early followers, both in word and action (his *sunna*, i.e. his customs and way of life), that provides Muslims with many of the detailed instructions for their religious practice and daily life.

The traditions were passed on orally for some generations, and eventually (not less than 150 years after Muhammad's death) they were gathered together and written down by a number of Muslim scholars. Each scholar made his own collection, and each *hadith* has a chain of names recording who had passed on the story. Some traditions are considered more reliable than others. According to Sunni Muslims, there are six authoritative collections. The Shia have their own separate collections. (See p. 103-5 for the difference between Sunni and Shia.)

Because the *ahadith* are often easier to understand than the Quran, they have played a very important role in establishing the rules of how Muslims should live. For example, the Quran tells Muslims to pray, but it is from the *ahadith* that Muslims know how often to pray, what time of day to pray and how to pray.

Two

Islamic Beliefs and Practices

FAITH AND WORKS

The religion of Islam demands of its believers firstly *iman* [faith], which Muslim theologians define as 'confession with the tongue and belief with the heart'. This confession runs: 'I testify that there is no god except Allah and that Muhammad is the Apostle (Messenger) of God.' This statement is known as the *shahada* or *kalima*.

The second requirement is for *din* [religion], in the sense of 'works' or practical duties. There are five of these, and because of their fundamental importance they are known as *arkan-ud-din* [the pillars of religion]. These are described in detail in chapter 4.

THE SIX ARTICLES OF FAITH

The six articles of faith in which Muslims must believe are:

1. *God [Allah]*

The unity of Allah is clearly taught in the Quran. Like the Bible, the Quran does not argue for the existence of God. It assumes that Allah is. The oneness of Allah is the first article of the *kalima*: 'There is no god but

Allah [*la ilah ill Allahu*].' This negative assertion is found frequently in the Quran. Similarly there is the repeated affirmation that *shirk*, the 'association of partners with Allah', is the worst of sins. Allah is one, having no equal and no partner. Omnipotence and omniscience are ascribed to Allah and are thought to safeguard both his unity and his majesty.

The word 'Allah' is the Arabic word for God and is used also by Arab Christians. There is much dispute as to whether Christians should use this term for 'God'; in Malaysia they are legally prohibited from doing so. It is important to recognise that the Muslim understanding of Allah is vastly different from the Christian understanding of God.

2. Angels [*malaikah*]
Angels are frequently mentioned in the Quran. They are created beings, made of light, and are referred to as 'messengers of Allah' with specific functions. They watch over humans and some record their deeds, both good and bad.

After death it is believed that most Muslims will suffer 'the torments of the grave' (*adhab al-qabr*). Two angels sit the corpse up and ask it, 'Who is your lord, what is your religion, who is your prophet?' A Muslim should answer, "Allah, Islam, Muhammad' and should therefore go directly to paradise and so avoid the torments. But this cannot be guaranteed because of a Quranic verse (Q 14:27) indicating that Allah will lead astray those who have led an unjust life. This results in fatalism and makes all Muslims afraid of having to endure the torments of the grave.

The torments, which all infidels and some Muslims will suffer, are very specific. First the angels pulverise the body with a huge iron hammer. Next the grave tightens around the corpse till its bones crack and the soul inside is suffocated. Thirdly a tomb-snake (or multiple snakes or dragons) eats the flesh, which re-grows again only to be eaten again. The screams of the tormented dead can be heard by all creation except humans and jinn.

It is small wonder that many Muslims are desperately afraid of these torments and seek a way to avoid them. There are three options for ensuring a direct transit to paradise without being tormented: to die on a Friday, to die of stomach ache, or to die as a martyr. Therefore in practical terms, becoming a suicide bomber is the one sure way to avoid the torments of the grave.

Angels are also believed to surround the throne of Allah to sing his praise. The greatest is Jibrail [Gabriel] the revealer of Allah to Muhammad, who is also called *Rul ul'Amin*, the Holy Spirit. It is he, say Muslims, who strengthened Jesus as well as bringing the Quran to Muhammad. The other archangels include Mikhail [Michael] the provider, Israfil the trumpeter of doom, and Izrail the custodian who has the care of the faithful at death.

It is important for Christians to remember that Quranic teaching specifically contradicts central Christian revelation (see pp. 46-50). Therefore a Christian must doubt whether the angel Gabriel of the Bible, who brought the message of Christ's birth to Mary and clearly declared Him to be the Son of the

Most High God, could declare some 600 years later
such a contradictory message.

Contrasted with the angels are the jinn, some
good, some evil. They were created by Allah out of
smokeless fire before he created Adam out of clay
(Q 15:26). These shadowy spirits frequent ruined
houses, desert places, and certain mountains and
wells. Many Muslims live in dread of evil jinn and take
various precautions to protect themselves from attack.

The devil, whose name is Iblis or Shaytan [Satan],
is sometimes described as a jinn and sometimes as
an angel.

3.   Books [kutub]

Muslims believe that Allah has revealed his commands to men through his prophets and through 104
sacred books. Of these books, only four now remain,
believed to have been given to Moses (the *Taurah*, i.e.
the Pentateuch), David (the *Zabur*, the Psalms), Jesus
(the *Injil*, the Gospels or the New Testament in general) and Muhammad (the Quran). It is claimed that
Jews and Christians, described jointly as *ahl-al-kitab*
[the people of the book], changed and distorted their
own Scriptures, so Allah sent the Quran as the final
revelation to mankind, thereby making all previous
scriptures obsolete.

4.   Prophets [nabi]

Through prophets Allah has mercifully deigned
to intervene in human history, in order to remind
humans of the last day and the life hereafter and to
guide them in all activities of life to the right path that

leads towards final election. The same truths were
revealed by the earlier prophets before Muhammad's
arrival. He links up with the faith of Abraham and
ends the recurring gaps between the prophets. As the
final messenger, he is often referred to as 'the seal
of the prophets'.

A Muslim cannot deny any of the prophets of the
Old Testament or John the Baptist and Jesus in the
New Testament (Q 2:285). Of the many prophets, only
nine are regarded as major prophets. These are Noah,
Abraham, David, Jacob, Joseph, Job, Moses, Jesus and
Muhammad. Muslims think that some of the Biblical
references to the coming Holy Spirit were prophecies
about Muhammad. The list of Islamic prophets also
includes many characters not found in the Bible, in
fact not known anywhere else at all.

Muslims do not worship Muhammad or any of the
prophets but consider them examples and models for
mankind. They dislike being called 'Muhammadans'
because they are not worshippers of Muhammad, but
of Allah. None of the prophets is considered divine.
Nevertheless Muhammad is so greatly venerated by
some Muslims that they see him as a logos-like figure
similar to Christ – a sinless saviour, mediator and
intercessor.

5. *Day of judgment* [*yawm al-akhirah*] *and*
   resurrection after death [*basi bad al-maut*]
Whether a human will go finally to paradise or to hell
is decided only at the Day of Judgment. Until that
time, the dead are in an intermediate state, *barzakh*
[interval, partition] awaiting a final verdict.

The day of judgment is described vividly in the Quran and is closely connected with the resurrection. The day will be preceded by clear signs and natural catastrophes, the appearance of the Antichrist [*Dajjal*], tumults and seditions, commotion in heaven and earth (Q 101:1-5; 70:9-10), the darkening of the sun and moon (Q 75:8; 81:1) and Christ's second coming, as a Muslim (see p. 26). On the last day:

> The trumpet will (just)
> Be sounded, when all
> That are in the heavens
> And on earth will swoon,
> Except such as it will
> Please Allah (to exempt).
> Then will a second one
> Be sounded, when, behold,
> They will be standing
> And looking on! (Q 39:68)

After the resurrection people will wander about for forty years, during which time the books containing the records of their deeds kept by the recording angels will be given up. Then will follow the weighing of the deeds on the eschatological scales [*mizan*].

> Then those whose balance
> (Of good deeds) is heavy –
> They will attain salvation.
> But those whose balance
> Is light, will be those
> Who have lost their souls;
> In Hell will they abide. (Q 23:102, 103)

Then everybody, believers and unbelievers, has to cross a very narrow bridge [*sirat*]. Some good Muslims might go straight to paradise, but most will fall off the bridge into hell and have to spend some time there, suffering punishment for their evil deeds before finally going to paradise. The infidels will all fall into hell and remain there forever. Some *ahadith* indicate that most of those sent to hell will be women.

6.   *Allah's sovereign decrees – predestination* [*taqbir*] Allah is considered to have supreme power and sovereignty over all things, both good and bad. The duty of a human being is to submit to Allah's inscrutable will and accept his or her fate. The doctrine of absolute predestination is widespread (see p. 63). *Maktub* [it is written], *maqdur* [it is decided] and *kismat* [it is my lot] are expressions commonly used to express this fatalism.

SHARIA – ISLAMIC LAW

As stated above, Islamic teaching is derived not only from the Quran but also from the *hadith*. Where the Quran and *hadith* are silent on a particular subject, rules are derived by consensus of the religious leaders [*ijma*] and by analogous reasoning [*qiyas*]. The combination of Quran, *hadith, ijma* and *qiyas* have been used by Islamic scholars to create the immensely detailed body of rules and regulations known as the sharia, that is, Islamic law.

Four orthodox schools are recognised in Sunni Islam:

Hanafi: founded by Imam abu Hanifa (died 767)
Maliki: founded by Imam Malik ibn Anas
    (died 795)
Shafii: founded by Imam Muhammad bin Idris ash
    Shafii (died 820)
Hanbali: founded by Imam Ahmad ibn Hanbal
    (died 855)

The Shia version of Islamic law is very similar and does not differ more from the Sunni schools than they do from each other.

One of the most important differences between Islam and Christianity is the existence of this detailed body of religious law. It regulates not only every aspect of a Muslim's devotional and personal life, but also the governing of an Islamic state. Compiled at a time when Islam was very much in the ascendant politically and militarily, the sharia makes the assumption that political power lies in the hands of the conquering Muslims. There are many rules relating to non-Muslims, mainly Jews and Christians, who are called *dhimmi* and treated as a conquered and subjugated people. *Dhimmi* are considered second-class citizens and must adhere to a number of restrictions designed to reinforce this second-class status. They have to pay a special tax called *jizya*.

Another feature of the sharia are the draconian punishments for certain crimes, such as amputation for theft, stoning for adultery etc. There is a death sentence for any adult male Muslim who leaves the faith. This arose in the early Muslim community in a context of warfare and disloyalty to the Muslim state where apostasy was seen as treason. The punishment for a woman apostate is either imprisonment or death, according to which school of law is followed. Likewise, Muslims who deviate from accepted Islamic orthodoxy are traditionally punished with death for their heresy, although in modern times there is a move to abolish this practice.

The attitude of the sharia to women does not reflect modern Western concepts of equality. Like non-Muslims, women are considered of less value than Muslim men, and this is reflected in many rules concerning inheritance, compensation, legal testimony etc. They are restricted by numerous rules ensuring their modesty and preventing them from leading men astray.

It is often argued that the sharia was quite moderate and lenient by contemporary standards at the time of its creation in the eighth and ninth centuries. But it has remained unchanged since then, and is extremely harsh by modern Western standards, infringing many areas of human rights, including the right to choose one's faith.

The strict sanctions against any who deviate from the existing rules have ensured that the sharia has survived unchanged for eleven centuries. The question of whether and how much it can be changed and adapted for the modern world is one that is debated within Islam today. The rise of radical Islam, which began in the middle of the twentieth century and continues now in the twenty-first, has made this debate a dangerous one for moderates who advocate change and liberalisation. They are liable to be condemned as heretics or apostates and assassinated.

No country of the world today rules according to the full sharia. However, many contain elements of it within their legislation. For example, the rule that apostates from Islam should be executed is part of the state law in Saudi Arabia and Sudan, to name but two countries.

Even where sharia is not legally enforced, the attitudes behind it are very prevalent amongst the Muslim community. Christian minorities in Muslim-majority contexts are commonly despised and discriminated against by society at large. They may find it hard to gain examination passes, get a job, get promotion or get justice from the police and judiciary. They are thought of and treated as *dhimmi*, even if the constitution and laws supposedly guarantee the equality of all citizens. Similarly, the position of women shows the influence of sharia on culture, even without legal enforcement.

The sharia's teaching that apostasy from Islam is a dreadful crime results in terrible shame being felt by a Muslim family if one of their members converts to Christianity. There will normally be rejection of the convert and sometimes violence, even murder, in accordance with the sharia's death penalty for an apostate. In Muslim countries, the law-enforcement officers are likely to sympathise with the murderer's motives, and therefore the murderer may be punished only lightly, if at all.

The ultimate goal of Muslim radicals is to introduce full sharia as widely as possible in the world, and thus create an Islamic state similar to that in Medina in Muhammad's time.

TAQIYYA [dissimulation]

The doctrine of *taqiyya* was first developed by Shia Muslims for dealing with persecution. It allowed Muslims to save their lives by concealing their true beliefs. It was later extended to allow such deception in order to save not just life but also honour or property. Eventually what had originally been meant only for emergencies became effectively normal, in both Shia and Sunni Islam.

The general principle is derived from Q 16:106 and Q 2:195. The detailed rules come from a number of *ahadith* that permit lying in the following three situations: (1) a man may lie to his wife to please her; (2) to bring reconciliation between two parties who have quarrelled; (3) in war, espionage etc.

The last of these – war – is often interpreted very broadly as any kind of defence of Islam. So many Muslims feel themselves completely justified in lying to non-Muslims about the nature of their faith. They sincerely believe that they are doing right by presenting an edited, sanitised version of Islam and Islamic history to non-Muslims because by glossing over the faults of their faith they are defending it against criticism.

The re-writing of history

Some Muslims have embarked on what appears to be a deliberate plan to enlarge and elevate the place of Islam in every academic discipline. An extensive publication programme supports this enterprise. Part of the plan is to revise text books in the West by introducing Islam and the 'Islamic legacy' to the West. The take-home message is that all that is best in European civilisation was derived from Islam and that Islamic history itself was completely peaceful and blameless.

Those engaged in this re-writing of history make false or exaggerated claims about the Islamic influence on medicine, science and architecture. They claim that Napoleon Bonaparte converted to Islam, that Muslim explorers reached America before Christopher Columbus, that Islam arrived in Australia in the ninth century and that an eighth-century king of Mercia (in the British Midlands) was a Muslim. They also claim that the rapid spread of Islam in its early years was peaceful and not imposed by force, while the Crusades were an unprovoked European assault on the peace-loving Muslim inhabitants of the Holy Land.

JESUS IN ISLAM

Jesus has a prominent place in the Quran. He is referred to as 'Son of Mary' or 'Jesus, son of Mary', and four times as 'the Messiah [Christ], son of Mary'. Though regarded as a prophet sent from Allah, his deity and atoning death are strenuously denied. Some interpreters of the Quran maintain that he did not die, but rather that Allah frustrated the plans of the Jews by allowing another man to be crucified in his place. Muslims believe that Jesus will come back to earth as a Muslim, will marry and have children, then die and be buried near Muhammad. Some traditions assert that at this second coming he will destroy every cross, convert the Christians to Islam, and reign as king of all Muslims.

(See also the Quran's affirmations and denials about Christ, pp. 50-7.)

THE 'GOSPEL' OF BARNABAS

A Christian discussing matters of faith with a Muslim may find their friend alluding to the 'Gospel of Barnabas'. This document is believed by many Muslims to contain the ultimate truth about the life and teaching of Jesus. Some even hold that it is the true and original *Injil*, for which Christians later substituted the New Testament.

The book professes to be a gospel written by the Apostle Barnabas. The author also claims that he, Barnabas, was one of the twelve disciples of Jesus, for which there is no support in the real Gospels. Furthermore, his denunciation of the Apostle Paul's teachings discounts the close and supportive relationship which existed between Paul and Barnabas according to the New Testament. The book denies that Jesus is the Son of God and portrays Him as a fore-runner (like John the Baptist) who proclaimed the future coming of Muhammad. It also denies the crucifixion. In addition, it even contradicts the Quran by declaring that Muhammad will be the Messiah, whereas the Gospels and Quran agree that this title belongs to Jesus alone. Such evidence, along with geographical and historical errors, shows that the Barnabas of the New Testament is not the author of this book.

Various references in the 'Gospel of Barnabas' point to its having been written in the Middle Ages, not earlier than the fourteenth century, i.e. well over a thousand years after Christ and 700 years after

Muhammad. The book contains most of the stories found in the four Gospel accounts in the New Testament, but with many things artfully turned in favour of Islam. A general study of its contents and authorship shows that it is a clumsy attempt to forge a life of Jesus that agrees with the profile of him in the Quran and Islamic tradition.

An English translation of the 'Gospel of Barnabas' by Lonsdale and Laura Ragg was reprinted in Pakistan in the 1970s and circulated in large numbers.

For further reading see John Gilchrist's *Origins and Sources of the Gospel of Barnabas*.

THE MUSLIM CALENDAR

This calendar was adopted by Muslims in about A.D. 632. The starting point (year 1) is the *hijra*, which occurred on 16th July 622 in the Christian calendar. Years are designated 'A.H.' for 'after *hijra*'.

The years are purely lunar and consist of twelve months containing in alternate sequence 30 or 29 days, with occasional adjustments of an additional day at the end of the twelfth month. The year is thus only 354 days long. The ninth month in each Muslim year (Ramadan) is observed as a fast. The pilgrimage to Mecca must be made in the twelfth month. The names of the Islamic months are as follows:

Muharram
Safar
Rabi al-awwal
Rabi al-thani
Jumada al-ula

Jumada al-akhirah
Rajab
Shaban
Ramadan
Shawal
Dhul qadah
Dhul hijjah

Because of its short length, the Muslim year starts about eleven days earlier each time. The regular annual festivals therefore occur on a different date each year in the Christian calendar.

RITES OF PASSAGE

The following practices are common in Islamic piety to mark important moments in the lives of Muslims. For example:

* *Birth* – when a baby is born the *adhan* is recited into the baby's right ear by the father.
* *Naming* – when the baby is seven days old (or later), the family sacrifices a sheep (one for a girl, two for a boy), and the meat is shared with family, visitors and the poor. The baby's head is shaved, the hair weighed and its weight in silver given to the poor.
* *Circumcision* – a boy is circumcised on or after seven days old, although this can be done any time up to puberty.
* *Bismillah ceremony* – this occurs around the fourth birthday. The child will have learnt to recite the first chapter of the Quran and will be taught to pray. This is the start of the child's Muslim education.

- *Marriage* – the wedding ceremony takes place either at the mosque or in the home and is usually led by the imam, with readings from the Quran, prayers and an exchange of vows. The *nikah* (contract) is signed, which defines the husband and wife's rights and responsibilities. This is followed by a party and feasting.

- *Death* – the dying person asks for blessing and forgiveness from Allah and from relatives and repeats the *shahada*. After death, the body is washed three times, anointed with spices and wrapped in sheets of white, unsewn cloth. The funeral is held on the day of the death, and includes prayers for the deceased and the family and readings from the Quran. The body is buried facing Mecca. During the mourning period well-wishers visit and provide food. Graves are visited at festival times.

RELATING TO NON-MUSLIMS

Jihad

The word 'jihad', which literally means 'struggle' or 'striving', has a variety of meanings in Islam. Firstly, it can mean the spiritual struggle for moral purity. Secondly, it can mean trying to correct wrong and support right by words and actions. Thirdly, it can mean an armed struggle in the name of Allah. The armed struggle may be against non-Muslims with the aim of spreading Islam, or against those who have left Islam, or against Muslims with unorthodox theology. This all-embracing struggle for Islamic rule includes offering one's time, property, health and life for Islam. According to sharia, jihad is one of the most basic religious duties.

Classical Islamic teaching divides the world into two parts. The House of Islam (*Dar al-Islam*) is where Muslims hold political power, and the rest of the world is called the House of War (*Dar al-Harb*). The alarming name for the non-Muslim part of the world signifies that Muslims are required to go to war with non-Muslims with the aim of conquering and subduing them, gradually adding their territory to the House of Islam. This kind of war is known as 'jihad'. In classical Islam, the caliph was required to lead an army in jihad against unbelievers at least once a year, and in the early years this was normal practice.

The doctrine of jihad developed gradually as Muhammad and the first Muslim community moved from a position of weakness to one of strength. Its development can be traced in the Quran. Early verses of the Quran urged non-confrontation (Q 16:125-128); later defensive fighting was allowed (Q 2:191); then it was permitted to initiate attacks on pagans (Q 2:191) and finally came commands to fight all unbelievers (Q 9:5), not just pagans but Jews and Christians as well (Q 9:29). It is the final stage in the development of this doctrine that inspires Islamist militants today, just as it did the conquering Muslim armies of old.

Sacred space

Territory has a spiritual importance in Islam. The Muslim teaching, which could be called the doctrine of 'sacred space', declares that all lands belong to

Allah, who has given them to the Muslims as an
inheritance. Some they already possess; the rest are
theirs in theory and will gradually become theirs in
practice. All conquered lands belong for ever to the
Muslim *umma* (nation), and Muslim-dominated areas
must never be allowed to fall again into the hands of
non-Muslims. This is applied on any scale from the
use of a church hall for Islamic prayer meetings to the
continuing resentment of the loss of Islamic Spain or
the presence of the modern state of Israel. Mosques,
once built, become sacred spaces that may never be
given up or demolished.

In the modern West, many non-violent methods
are used to gain control of territory, though some
radicals advocate the use of traditional jihad. The
laws and practices of Western and other non-Islamic
societies are increasingly being adapted to conform
with sharia and with Muslim sensibilities, as the first
step in creating a parallel society and then winning
political and legal control for Islam. At a spiritual
level, Muslims hold processions round areas of cities, even in the West, chanting the names of Allah,
in order to Islamise the streets and buildings. Local
mosques are also considered to be places of spiritual
influence, which extends to a certain distance around
the building. Muslims seek to buy and live in all the
surrounding houses, effectively creating a sacred
space, purely Muslim.

A further strategy is the use of demographic
change. This can include Muslim migration (*hijra*)
to non-Muslim countries or parts of countries. It also
includes the high birth rate of Muslim populations

compared with that of non-Muslims. These strategies are seen as a means of gaining control through sheer weight of numbers.

Dawa

Dawa is the Islamic term for missionary outreach that aims to convert people to Islam. It literally means a 'call' or 'invitation' to Islam and covers not only the conversion of individuals to personal faith but also the conversion of whole societies to Islamic structures and practices, e.g. Islamic finance. Thus it is closely linked to jihad, with each helping the other as different parts of the same enterprise.

Dawa is a duty not just for individual Muslims but also for Muslim states, who must follow Muhammad's example by converting non-Islamic states to Islam. Intensive *dawa* activities are taking place in non-Muslim parts of the world today, involving many people and often financed by seemingly limitless oil wealth from Saudi Arabia, the Gulf States, Libya and Iran. In poor regions, such as some parts of Africa, material rewards are often offered as inducements to convert. In the West, attractive half-truths about Islam are often presented, without mention of the death sentence for leaving Islam. Marriage is also used both in the West and in the non-Western world as a means of gaining converts.

ARAB-MUSLIM ORIGINS

The Arab people have a place of special respect within Islam because they are mother-tongue speakers of the language of the Quran. One consequence of this is that non-Arab Muslims today are being 'Arabised', in places as diverse as Africa and Indonesia.

The early history of the Arab people is obscure. Muslims, however, have well-defined traditions that divide them into two main groupings, based in the north and the south of the Arabian Peninsula. The southerners are believed to be descended from the Biblical Joktan (Qahtan), who was a descendant of Noah and (according to Muslim belief) became the first king of Yemen. The northerners are believed to be descended from the Biblical Ishmael (Ismail), Abraham's son. Muhammad and his tribe, the Quraysh, claimed descent from Ishmael. The southerners considered themselves 'pure Arabs', while the northerners were held to be 'mixed Arabs'.

There are no real historical records of ancient times that can corroborate these Muslim Arab claims. It is likely that they were invented later, during the early Islamic era. Later they were used to justify the supremacy of the Arabs amongst Muslims.

It is interesting to note that Genesis 10 mentions descendants of Noah's sons Ham (Sheba, Dedan) and Shem (Joktan, Hazarmaveth, Sheba, Uzal), whose names correspond to areas and tribes of the Arabian Peninsula. This suggests that Arabia was already populated with the descendants of Ham and Shem long before Ishmael was born. In the light of this, the theory that all Arabs are descended from Ishmael is highly questionable.

Quranic stories about Abraham and Ishmael living in Mecca and building the Kaaba have no external corroboration from any sources.

The Old Testament records that Ishmael's twelve sons moved to the southern part of the Syrian desert (Gen. 25:12-18). They most likely intermarried with the local population and produced the various nomadic tribes known as Ishmaelites, which are mentioned in Assyrian records. They are also called Hagarites in the Bible. They did not settle as far south as Mecca. In Judges 8:22-24, the Midianites are equated with the Ishmaelites, so it is likely that the two had intermingled. The Arabs are mentioned in the Old Testament as a distinct tribe, separate from the Ishmaelites, Midianites etc. For example in Nehemiah 4:7 they appear as allies of the Ammonites.

After the founding of Islam, and after it had gained control of the Arabian Peninsula and the Levant, Arabisation and Islamisation gradually integrated all the local tribes and settled populations into the Islamic-Arabic culture. These included tribes and populations descended from Abraham's other wife Keturah (Midian, Medan), and others descended from Lot (Ammon, Moab), from Esau (Edomites) and from the Canaanite nations.

The historic indigenous Christian populations of many Muslim-majority countries now considered to be Arab strongly affirm that they are *not* Arabs. For example, Egyptian Christians are Copts, descended from the Pharaonic peoples, Iraqi Christians are Assyrians, and Lebanese Christians trace their ancestry to the Phoenicians.

Three

The Quran

INTRODUCTION

The Quran, the sacred book of the Muslims, is believed by them to have been revealed to Muhammad by the angel Gabriel 'piecemeal' as occasion required during the last twenty-three years of his life. Muslims take a fundamentalist attitude to God's word, and the Quran holds a place of exalted reverence in their hearts. They believe it to be the word of Allah in the most literal sense, and that it cannot be compared with any human writing. They claim that Muhammad was merely the recipient of that word and passed it on as an exact copy of an uncreated original in heaven. It bears no imprint of the prophet's character at all, and Muslims consider it blasphemous to attribute the Quran even in a secondary sense to Muhammad, as, for example, the writings of the Bible are attributed to their human authors.

Muslims believe that the Quran was miraculously revealed to guide believers in the right path and that it supersedes all earlier revealed scriptures. They also hold that it has been perfectly preserved over the centuries. Most Muslims today would not believe that many different versions of the Quran were once in circulation. In Muslim theology the Quran has a place similar to that of Christ in Christianity, as the eternal, uncreated word of God.

The Quran plays a special part in the lives of most Muslims, who have to recite a section or verses from it five times every day in their prayers, and try to learn by heart as many verses as possible. No pious Muslim would ever drink, smoke, or make a noise while the Quran is being read aloud. The chanting of the Quran in Arabic has a pleasing - even hypnotic - effect on the Arabic-speaking person; this cannot be conveyed in an English translation.

Although it does not deal with all aspects of life for which Islam legislates, Muslims believe that in those areas in which the Quran speaks it does so with absolute divine authority, and that it is their primary source of authority.

ORIGINS

Muslims believe that the Quran exists eternally in heaven, engraved in Arabic on a stone tablet. There-fore the Arabic language is thought superior to any other language, and speakers of Arabic have a special prestige in the eyes of the Muslim world. The language is held to be of such importance that when Muslim children are taught the Quran the primary aim is to train them to read it aloud in Arabic (or preferably to recite it from memory in Arabic). Understanding what the words mean is less important (especially for girls). It is ironic that many of the words in the Quran (not to mention stories and names) are actually derived from Aramaic, the language of Jesus, which was the main language of the region until the rise of Islam.

The 'revelations' were passed on orally by Muhammad to his companions; some wrote them down, and others memorised them. Muslim orthodoxy holds that the angel Gabriel helped Muhammad to put the revelations together from time to time so that at his death there was an exact transcript of what was written on the heavenly tablet.

Modern scholarship however has shown that there was no complete set of collated and arranged revelations at Muhammad's death, and that an editorial process seems to have taken place. Some time after his death the revelations were assembled by Muslim leaders from records written on leaves, stones, camel's shoulder-blades etc. and from the memories of those who had stored the revelations in their minds. The resulting collections of revelations made in different places varied somewhat from each other. Caliph Uthman decided to bring order to the situation and had scholars create an official standard text between 650 and 656, which he circulated widely while ordering all other versions to be destroyed.

The oldest surviving fragments of Quranic manuscripts date from no earlier than the second century A.H. (approximately the eighth century A.D.). They are written in a Kufic script showing consonants only. The result is as ambiguous and open to interpretation as if all the vowels and punctuation marks were to be removed from an English text. Vowel points and other helpful marks were added later. Variants continued to exist until at least the tenth century A.D., when some Islamic scholars were imprisoned for refusing to abandon their preferred versions. Even in the mid-twentieth century two versions were still in use, a fact that would be disbelieved by most Muslims. While the majority of the Muslim world had one version, an alternative was still in use in North Africa, though it was rapidly being ousted by the main version. The Muslim argument that Christians have changed their Scriptures while Muslims have not is therefore clearly inaccurate according to the evidence.

STRUCTURE AND CONTENT

The Quran is about the same length as the New Testament, and is divided into 114 suras (chapters). The suras are not arranged in chronological order but in order of decreasing length (apart from sura 1, which is very short).

It is essential for anyone trying to understand the message of the Quran to know something about the dating of the various chapters. Because some of the verses contradict other verses, Muslim scholars have devised rules as to which verse to follow in cases of conflicting teaching. The most widely used rule states that a later verse abrogates [cancels] an earlier verse. The rationale for this is that the earlier verse was appropriate to the early stages of Muhammad's mission, but later, different conditions required it to be modified. Following this rule is not always easy because scholars are not in total agreement about the dating of all the verses. However, it is useful to know at least which chapters were revealed earlier, when Muhammad was living in Mecca, and which were revealed later, after he had moved to Medina. (See Appendix 3)

The first five verses of sura 96 are generally regarded as the earliest revelation. They begin 'Proclaim! (or read!) in the name of thy Lord and Cherisher ...' It is from the first word, *iqra* [proclaim, read, recite], that the word 'Quran' is derived.

Sura 1 is used by Muslims as a prayer, and has a similar place in Islam to the Lord's Prayer in the life of a Christian. It runs:

> Praise be to Allah
> The Cherisher and Sustainer of the Worlds;
> Most Gracious, Most Merciful;
> Master of the Day of Judgment.
> Thee do we worship,
> And Thine aid we seek.
> Show us the straight way,
> The way of those on whom
> Thou hast bestowed Thy Grace,
> Those whose (portion)
> Is not wrath,
> And who go not astray.

It is recited many times a day by devout Muslims who are faithful in performing the required prayers. Some English translations explain in brackets that those on whom God's wrath rests are the Jews and that those who go astray are the Christians. This is the traditional understanding of the passage.

The earliest suras bear some comparison to the psalms in length, subject matter and rhythmic form. They differ in approach, however, as they are not the yearning of the human heart for God, but Allah speaking to humankind and using Muhammad as a mouthpiece.

The Quran contains many warnings of the coming Day of Judgment, and it describes paradise and hell. It criticises Jews and Christians and attacks their beliefs, stressing the unity and greatness of Allah, the importance of Muhammad as his messenger and the duty to obey him. Several hundred verses set out regulations for the life of the Muslim community – liturgical, legal and social. Various pagan beliefs are included, for example, reverence for the Kaaba at Mecca. The Quran also has stories of Biblical characters, especially Joseph and Jesus but also Moses and some others. These stories differ from the Biblical versions, suggesting that their source was not the Bible directly but secondary (and perhaps heretical) Jewish and Christian sources. The Quran does not tell the story of Muhammad's life.

TRANSLATIONS

Because the Arabic language of the original Quran is held in such reverence, versions in other languages are seen as only approximations and paraphrases. Some are given titles hinting that something may have been lost in translation, such as 'The Meaning of the Glorious Quran' or 'The Interpretation of the Meaning of the Glorious Quran'.

Many translations have been given a particular 'spin' by the translators. Because the original Arabic text is ambiguous and hard to understand, any translations that seem clear and comprehensible have certainly had a considerable amount of editorial input. This is sometimes clearly visible: the editors' explanations are shown in brackets, footnotes, appendices etc. Some versions appear to be 'straight' translation without editorial additions or interpretations, but are probably not.

The bias introduced in translation can go in various directions. Some modern English translations are specifically designed to present Islam in an attractive way for Western readers. These translations moderate the more violent verses. For example, the 'Sword Verse' (Q 9:5) appears in Fazlollah Nikayin's translation of the Quran, published in 2000, as:

> And when the sacred months are over,
> Fight the idolaters unto the finish

This compares with a more standard translation, such as Yusuf Ali's:

> But when the forbidden months are past,
> then fight them and slay the Pagans

Other modern translations go to the opposite extreme and are being used to promote radical Islam around the world. The Saudi government is funding the distribution of millions of copies of a translation by Muhammad Taqi-ud-Din Al-Hilali and Muhammad Muhsin Khan that makes very clear their belief that jihad should be understood as literal, physical warfare.

> And make ready against them all you can of power, including steeds of war (tanks, planes, missiles, artillery) to threaten the enemy of Allah and your enemy, and others besides whom, you may not know but whom Allah does know. (Q 8:60)

In this book I am quoting from a translation by Abdullah Yusuf Ali, which first appeared in 1934 and pre-dates the contemporary tendency to impose strong editorial bias. Yusuf Ali's translation takes a traditional, middle-of-the-spectrum understanding of the text and was very widely used until the Saudi government began to spread Al-Hilali and Khan's translation.

THE TESTIMONY OF THE QURAN TO ITSELF

It will be noted from the following selections, representative of many other verses in the Quran, that the Quran repeatedly asserts that it is a revelation direct from Allah. The following verses were 'revealed' to Muhammad in reply to objections that it was he who had produced it.

> Say: 'If the whole
> Of mankind and Jinns
> Were to gather together
> To produce the like
> Of this Quran they
> Could not produce
> The like thereof, even if
> They backed up each other
> With help and support.' (Q 17:88)

> This Quran is not such
> As can be produced
> By other than Allah;
> On the contrary it is
> A confirmation of (revelations)
> That went before it,
> And a fuller explanation

> Of the Book – wherein
> There no doubt –
> From the Lord of the Worlds.
> Or do they say, 'He forged it'?
> Say: 'Bring then
> A Surah like unto it,
> And call (to your aid)
> Anyone you can,
> Besides Allah, if it be
> Ye speak the truth!' (Q 10:37, 38)

The reference to the fact of the Quran verifying what came before it (Q 10:37) is another frequently asserted claim for the Quran, i.e. that it confirms and carries on the revelation previously 'sent down' in the *Taurah* and the *Injil*. Typical of such claims is the following verse:

> It is He [Allah] Who sent down
> To thee (step by step),
> In truth, the Book,
> Confirming what went before it;
> And He sent down the Law
> (Of Moses) and the Gospel (Of Jesus)
> Before this, as a guide to mankind. (Q 3:3)

In reply to the contention by some of Muhammad's opponents that there were obvious contradictions in the Quran, a verse was revealed to settle the matter:

> Allah doth blot out
> Or confirm what He pleaseth:
> With Him is
> The Mother of the Book (Q 13:39)

This is the famous 'verse of abrogation', justifying
the practice of letting the later-dated verse annul
the earlier. The 'Mother of the Book', i.e. the source
of revelation, refers to the eternal original kept in
heaven.

One further claim of the Quran for itself should
be noticed, namely, that it was revealed in Arabic,
the language of the people to whom it was sent down,
and not in a foreign language, like the *Taurah* of the
Jews and the *Injil* of the Christians:

> Alif Lam Ra. These are
> The Symbols (or Verses)
> Of the Perspicuous Book.
> We have sent it down
> As an Arabic Quran,
> In order that ye may
> Learn wisdom. (Q 12:1, 2)

THE TESTIMONY OF THE QURAN TO PREVIOUS HOLY BOOKS

There are over 120 references in the Quran to the
Scriptures of the Jews and the Christians, testifying
to their being genuine revelations from Allah. The
Jews and Christians were generally known as 'the
people of the Book'.

It is important that Christians relating to Muslims
should know that Muhammad did not claim to bring
a completely new revelation, or to establish a new
religion. His concern was to bring his people back to
the original religion professed and preached by all the

prophets from Adam onwards. The following verse is
an illustration of this attitude:

> Say ye: 'We believe
> In Allah, and the revelation
> Given to us, and to Abraham,
> Ismail, Isaac, Jacob,
> And the Tribes, and that given
> To Moses and Jesus, and that given
> To (all) Prophets from their Lord:
> We make no difference
> Between one and another of them:
> And we bow to Allah (in Islam).' (Q 2:136)

Typical of verses that indicate the acceptance by
Muhammad of the existing holy books is that found in
Q 4:163

> We have sent thee
> Inspiration, as We sent it
> To Noah and the Messengers
> After him: We sent
> Inspiration to Abraham,
> Ismail, Isaac, Jacob
> And the Tribes, to Jesus,
> Job, Jonah, Aaron and Solomon,
> And to David We gave
> The Psalms.

Muhammad's dependence on the holy books is even
more clearly indicated in Q 10:94, which recommends
consulting the Jews and Christians 'who have been
reading the book from before thee':

> If thou wert in doubt
> As to what We have revealed

Unto thee, then ask those
Who have been reading
The Book from before thee.

The Christian is, therefore, in a very strong position
in inviting the Muslim to read the Scriptures, for the
Quran clearly testifies to their authenticity, and even
advises the perplexed Muslim to consult the Christians about matters of religion that he or she does not
understand. At this point, however, a barrier arises
between the Muslim and the Christian. Any Muslim
who did in fact consult a Christian, or read the Christian Scriptures, would find obvious contradictions to
the teaching of the Quran.

This is a serious problem to the Muslim, for if the
Quran and the other books – the *Taurah, Zabur* and
Injil – are all from Allah, and if the Quran is a confir-
mation of the message of the earlier books, then there
should be harmony and continuity, not contradiction.
The only honest conclusion that can be arrived at from
the existence of contradictions is that either the previous Scriptures are not in fact revelations from Allah
or the Quran is not in fact a revelation from Allah.
But that is quite contrary to the plain teaching of the
Quran. To escape from this dilemma Muslims have
introduced the theory of the corruption of the existing
copies of the Scriptures of the Jews and Christians.
According to this theory, the references in the Quran
to the previous Scriptures are to the original books,
and not to the present 'corrupt' copies. In support
of this theory, the following verse from the Quran is
sometimes quoted:

There is among them
A section who distort
The Book with their tongues:
(As they read) you would think
It is a part of the Book,
But it is no part
Of the Book; and they say,
'That is from Allah',
But it is not from Allah:
It is they who tell
A lie against Allah,
And (well) they know it! (Q 3:78)

One illustration of how this alleged corruption occurred is the Muslim contention that the Biblical
reference in John 16:7 (and other places) to the
coming of the Holy Spirit as Counsellor was originally
a prophecy concerning the coming of Muhammad,
another form of whose name is 'Ahmad'. The verse in
the Quran to which Muslims commonly refer in this
context reads:

And remember, Jesus,
The son of Mary, said:
'O Children of Israel!
I am the messenger of Allah
(Sent) to you, confirming
The Law (which came)
Before me, and giving
Glad Tidings of a Messenger
To come after me,
Whose name shall be Ahmad.' (Q 61:6)

The Muslim contention is that the Greek word *Para-
cletos* (translated 'Counsellor', 'Comforter' or similarly

in the Gospel) is a corruption of the original word
Periclutos, the meaning of which in Arabic is stated to
be 'Ahmad'. (For further reading, see John Gilchrist's
Is Muhammad Foretold in the Bible?)

This, and all other alleged corruptions of the Scriptures, can easily be shown to be without foundation,
from the simple fact that complete manuscripts of the
Greek New Testament, which go back two centuries or
more before the time of Muhammad, are in existence
today. These substantiate the text of our present-day
versions, and not the Quranic variant.

THE AFFIRMATIONS OF THE QURAN ABOUT CHRIST

The Quran makes a number of positive statements
about Christ. The following are some of its most important affirmations.

1. *The virgin birth*

Some of the longest chapters in the Quran are concerned with Jesus and Mary and the annunciation of
the birth of Christ. The following are some extracts:

> Behold! The angels said:
> 'O Mary! Allah giveth thee
> Glad tidings of a Word
> From Him, his name
> Will be Christ Jesus.
> The son of Mary, held in honour
> In this world and the Hereafter
> And of (the company of) those
> Nearest to Allah.' (Q 3:45)

> She said: 'O my Lord!
> How shall I have a son

When no man hath touched me?'
He said: 'Even so:
Allah createth
What He willeth:
When He hath decreed
A Plan, He but saith
To it, "Be," and it is!' (Q 3:47)

Other key passages on Mary are found in Q 19:16-17, 19-22 and Q 66:12.

2.   The assertion that Jesus is a created being

The similitude of Jesus
Before Allah is as that of Adam;
He created him from dust,
Then said to him: 'Be'
And he was. (Q 3:59)

Although the obvious intention of this verse is to establish the fact of Jesus' being merely a human, there could be some ambiguity as to whether the phrase 'He created him' refers to Adam or to Jesus. If the reference is to Adam, there is, of course, no contradiction of the Christian Scriptures here. It is generally regarded by Muslims, however, as referring to Jesus. In any case, this is a verse to which the Christian's best reply is to state that the Christian Scriptures also compare Jesus with Adam, not because He is a created being like Adam, but that, like Adam, He is the head of a new creation.

3.   The miracles
There is a good deal in the Quran (and still more in other Muslim writings) of the miracles Jesus

performed by way of authenticating His mission. But
they are always stated to be 'by the permission of
Allah'. There is no recognition of the fact that Christ
had any inherent divine power. The following verse
is a sample of these statements:

> Then will Allah say:
> 'O Jesus the son of Mary!
> Recount My favour
> To thee and to thy mother.
> Behold! I strengthened thee
> With the holy spirit,
> So that thou didst speak
> To the people in childhood
> And in maturity.
> Behold! I taught thee
> The Book and Wisdom,
> The Law and the Gospel.
> And behold! thou makest
> Out of clay, as it were,
> The figure of a bird,
> By My leave,
> And thou breathest into it,
> And it becometh a bird
> By My leave,
> And thou healest those
> Born blind, and the lepers,
> By My leave.
> And behold! thou
> Bringest forth the dead
> By My leave.' (Q 5:110)

THE DENIALS OF THE QURAN ABOUT CHRIST

The denials of the Quran relate to some of the most basic Christian doctrines concerning Christ. These carry great weight with a Muslim, who believes that they are the Word of Allah expressed in Allah's own words.

1. Denial of the Trinity and of the deity of Christ

> Christ Jesus the son of Mary
> Was (no more than)
> A Messenger of Allah,
> And His Word,
> Which He bestowed on Mary,
> And a Spirit proceeding
> From Him: so believe
> In Allah and His Messengers.
> Say not 'Trinity': desist:
> It will be better for you:
> For Allah is One God:
> Glory be to Him:
> (Far exalted is He) above
> Having a son. (Q 4:171)

> And behold! Allah will say:
> 'O Jesus the son of Mary!
> Didst thou say unto men,
> "Worship me and my mother
> As gods in derogation of Allah"?'
> He will say: 'Glory to Thee!
> Never could I say
> What I had no right
> (To say).' (Q 5:116)

It is well to note here that what the Muslim rejects as the false teaching of some Christian sects, the

Christian also rejects. For what Muhammad rejects here is not the true teaching of Christianity, but what he thought was its teaching. He understood the Christians to believe that the Trinity consisted of Father, Mother (Mary) and Son. Most likely it was the extreme veneration accorded to Mary by Christians whom Muhammad met that gave rise to this view.

2.   Denial of the Sonship of Christ

There are many verses in the Quran that stress the absolute unity of Allah, and by implication deny the Sonship of Christ, and there are others that deny the possibility of Sonship in general, such as sura 112, which runs in its entirety:

> Say: He is Allah,
> The One and Only;
> Allah, the Eternal, Absolute;
> He begetteth not
> Nor is He begotten;
> And there is none
> Like unto Him. (Q 112)

There are also a number of verses where the Sonship of Christ is specifically denied, such as Q 4:171, already quoted in connection with the Trinity, and the following verses:

> Such (was) Jesus the son
> Of Mary: (it is) a statement
> Of truth, about which
> They (vainly) dispute.
> It is not befitting
> To (the majesty of) Allah

> That He should beget
> A son. (Q 19:34, 35)

Another relevant passage is Q 6:101-6.

The seriousness of the Muslim view of the Christian doctrines of the Trinity and of the deity of Christ is seen in the following verse:

> Allah forgiveth not
> That partners should be set up
> With Him; but He forgiveth
> Anything else, to whom
> He pleaseth: to set up
> Partners with Allah
> Is to devise a sin
> Most heinous indeed. (Q 4:48)

This is the unpardonable sin of *shirk*. Although *shirk* – associating anyone with Allah as a co-deity – is the most deadly of all sins, what makes the Christian doctrine even more blasphemous in the eyes of a Muslim is the description of Christ as the Son of God. This arises from the fact that a Muslim – or more properly Muhammad – thinks of sonship only in terms of a sexual relationship between father and mother. It is probably true to say that a Muslim is less offended by our ascribing deity to Christ than by our calling Him the Son of God.

3.   Denial of the crucifixion of Christ
This is probably the best known and most basic of all Muslim denials about Christ, not least because it is so categorical.

> That they rejected Faith;
> That they uttered against Mary
> A grave false charge;
> That they said (in boast),
> 'We killed Christ Jesus
> The son of Mary,
> The Messenger of Allah'; –
> But they killed him not,
> Nor crucified him,
> But so it was made
> To appear to them ...
>
> For of a surety
> They killed him not –
> Nay, Allah raised him up
> Unto Himself; and Allah
> Is exalted in Power, Wise. (Q 4:156-158)

No Muslim can side-step the categorical denial of the death of Christ contained in this passage, in spite of the fact that it poses a serious difficulty for the thoughtful Muslim. If Christ did not die, that would obviously make him far superior to other prophets, such as Muhammad, who did die. But to believe he actually did die means denying the Word of Allah, or at least believing that it has been misinterpreted. To escape from this dilemma, Muslim traditions speak of the future return of Christ to this world, his embracing of Islam and his subsequent death. This position is based on an interpretation of verses such as the following:

> 'So Peace is on me
> The day I was born,

The day that I die,
And the day that I
Shall be raised up
To life (again)'!
Such (was) Jesus the son
of Mary. (Q 19:33-4)

The most obvious way to make this verse fit the theory
would be to alter the order of the words, so that the
phrase 'the day that I die' follows the phrase 'the day
that I shall be raised up to life', but such an alteration
would be sinful to a Muslim as it involves an alteration
to the revealed Word of Allah. It is, in any case, a weak
argument, as the very same words are used in verse 15
of the same sura, in connection with John the son of
Zechariah (John the Baptist), and no one would think
of altering the order of the words in this case.

THE TEACHING OF THE QURAN

The following are some of the other subjects that the
Quran speaks about.

1. The Fall

We said, 'O Adam! dwell thou
And thy wife in the Garden;
And eat of the bountiful things therein
As (where and when) ye will; but approach not
this tree
Or ye run into harm and transgression.'
Then did Satan make them slip
From the (Garden) and get them out
Of the state (of felicity) in which
They had been. We said:

'Get ye down, all (ye people),
With enmity between yourselves...' (Q 2:35-6)

See also Q 7:19ff. and 20:115-123. In this connection
it should be noted that the Quran knows nothing of
any earthly paradise in Eden. Paradise is in heaven,
and it was from heaven to earth that Adam and Eve
literally fell.

2. The Devil
The origin and works of Iblis or Shaytan, the devil,
are described in Q 7:11-18, which begins as follows:

It is We who created you
And gave you shape;
Then We bade the angels
Bow down to Adam, and they
Bowed down; not so Iblis
He refused to be of those
Who bow down.

(Allah) said: 'What prevented
Thee from bowing down
When I commanded thee?'
He said: 'I am better
Than he: Thou didst create
Me from fire, and him from clay.'

(Allah) said: 'Get thee down
From this: it is not
For thee to be arrogant
Here: get out, for thou
Art of the meanest (of creatures).'

3. Hell

Hell is a place of fiery torment for sinners.

> And what will explain
> To thee what Hell-Fire is?
> Naught doth it permit
> To endure, and naught
> Doth it leave alone! –
> Darkening and changing
> The colour of man! (Q 74:27-9)

Other passages describing hell and those who will go there include Q 50:24-6 and 78:21-30.

4. Heaven or paradise

The name most frequently given to paradise, the abode of the blessed, is *janna* [garden]. The description of paradise in the Quran shows that it is essentially a place of sensual delights in which there are beautiful women, couches covered with rich brocades, flowing cups and luscious fruits.

> (Other) faces that Day
> Will be joyful,
> Pleased with their Striving, –
> In a Garden on high
> Where they shall hear
> No (word) of vanity:
> Therein will be
> A bubbling spring:
> Therein will be Thrones
> (Of dignity) raised on high,
> Goblets placed (ready)
> And Cushions set in rows,

And rich carpets
(All) spread out." (Q 88:8-16)

Q 56:8-38 gives more details, including the following:

Round about them will (serve)
Youths of perpetual (freshness),
With goblets, (shining) beakers,
And cups (filled) out of
Clear-flowing fountains:
No after-ache will they
Receive therefrom, nor will they
Suffer intoxication:
And with fruits,
Any that they may select; –
And the flesh of fowls,
Any that they may desire.
And (there will be) Companions
With beautiful, big,
And lustrous eyes, –
Like unto Pearls
Well-guarded,
A Reward for the Deeds
Of their past (Life)...

We have created (their Companions)
Of special creation.
And made them
Virgin-pure (and undefiled), –
Beloved (by nature),
Equal in age –

5. Resurrection and Judgment

Eschatology forms a very large part of the teaching of
the Quran, especially in the early suras that reflect

Muhammad's early preaching at Mecca. There are
lengthy accounts of the resurrection and judgment
in suras 75; 81:1-19; 82; 83:4-21; 84.

> When the stars
> Fall, losing their lustre;
> When the mountains vanish
> (Like a mirage);
> When the she-camels,
> Ten months with young,
> Are left untended;
> When the wild beasts
> Are herded together
> (In human habitations);
> When the oceans
> Boil over with a swell;
> When the souls
> Are sorted out,
> (Being joined, like with like);
> When the female (infant),
> Buried alive, is questioned –
> For what crime
> She was killed;
> When the Scrolls
> Are laid open;
> When the World on High
> Is unveiled;
> When the Blazing Fire
> Is kindled to fierce heat;
> And when the Garden
> Is brought near –
> (Then) shall each soul know
> What it has put forward. (Q 81:2-14)

6. Forgiveness

There is very little in the Quran about forgiveness
in comparison with some other subjects, which are
dealt with at length. From what is mentioned, it
is clear that it is regarded as a quite arbitrary act
of Allah which has little, if any, moral basis, and
requires no act of redemption or reconciliation. The
following are some of the few verses dealing with
this subject:

> For those who reject Allah,
> Is a terrible Penalty: but
> For those who believe
> And work righteous deeds,
> Is Forgiveness, and
> A magnificent Reward. (Q 35:7)

> Allah forgiveth not
> that partners should be set up
> With Him; but He forgiveth
> Anything else to whom
> He pleaseth (Q 4:48)

Leaving aside the unpardonable sin of *shirk*, sins
are divided into great and little sins. The great
sins [*kabira*] originally included murder, adultery,
disobedience, usury, the neglect of Friday prayers
or the Ramadan fast, forgetting the Quran after
reading it, swearing falsely or by any other name
than that of Allah, the practice of magic, gambling,
dancing, and shaving the beard. Some of these are
no longer regarded as great sins. The little sins
[*saghira*] include such offences as lying, deception, anger and lust.

7. Predestination

Many Islamic traditions suggest that humans cannot be held responsible for their actions. Teaching on predestination is very closely linked with teaching on forgiveness, appearing in such verses as:

> For Allah leaves to stray
> Whom He wills, and guides
> Whom He wills. (Q 35:8)

The same sentiments are expressed in Q 6:39; 14:4; 74:31.

8. Prayer

A Muslim prays five times a day at set times. There is however no single verse in the Quran where all five prayer times are mentioned together. Prayer for a Muslim is much more of a religious exercise than prayer as a Christian knows it. Prayers must be said in Arabic, and the same forms and words are used every time. The following are some of the Quranic verses referring to prayer:

> And establish regular prayers
> At the two ends of the day
> And at the approaches of the night:
> For those things that are good
> Remove those that are evil. (Q 11:114)

> When ye pass
> (Congregational) prayers,
> Celebrate Allah's praises,
> Standing, sitting down,
> Or lying down on your sides;

But when ye are free
From danger, set up
Regular Prayers:
For such prayers
Are enjoined on Believers
At stated times. (Q 4:103)

Ceremonial ablutions must precede prayer.

O ye who believe!
When ye prepare
For prayer, wash
Your faces, and your hands
(And arms) to the elbows;
Rub your heads (with water);
And (wash) your feet
To the ankles. (Q 5:6)

9. Freedom of religion

Freedom of religion is a subject where there is
contradictory teaching within the Quran. A frequently quoted verse that is apparently in favour
of freedom of religion runs: 'Let there be no compulsion in religion' (Q 2:256). However, there is
a wide variety of interpretations of this verse in
classical Islam.

Muslims are clearly exhorted to 'fight and slay
the pagans wherever ye find them' (Q 9:5) and to
'fight those who believe not in Allah nor the Last
Day ... nor acknowledge the Religion of Truth, from
among the People of the Book, until they pay the
jizya with willing submission and feel themselves
subdued' (Q 9:29).

Because sura 9 post-dates sura 2, the rule of abrogation indicates that it is sura 9 that should be followed (whatever interpretation is given to Q 2:256). This was certainly the practice of early Muslims as they forcefully spread the new faith by means of jihad. It is fortunate that this attitude is found in only a minority of Muslims today. Nevertheless there are tragic examples of large-scale forced conversions to Islam in recent history. In the early twentieth century some 1.5 million Armenian and other eastern Christians were massacred by the Turks. At the turn of the twenty-first century many thousands of Indonesian Christians were forced to convert to Islam by 'jihad warriors' of many nationalities; any who refused were killed. Since the 2003 invasion of Iraq, Islamist militants have begun threatening Iraqi Christians with a four-fold choice: convert to Islam, pay *jizya*, leave, or be killed. Similar attitudes and threats are beginning to be reported from Pakistan.

In connection with the subject of freedom of worship, it is important to remember also the sharia's ruling that even if non-Muslim minorities are protected (i.e. not killed) and allowed to worship in their own way, they are still not granted equal rights with Muslims. (See *dhimmi*, pp. 22, 24)

The Quran does not clearly teach that apostates from Islam should be killed. It is ambiguous, and can be understood to say that their punishment will take place in the next life, not in this one.

10. Islam is the only religion acceptable to God

If anyone desires
A religion other than
Islam (submission to Allah),
Never will it be accepted
Of him; and in the Hereafter
He will be in the ranks
Of those who have lost
(All spiritual good). (Q 3:85)

Four

The Five Pillars of Islam

INTRODUCTION

Islam has a very highly developed code of religious observance, usually referred to as *arkan-ud-din* [pillars of religion]. This chapter describes the normal practices of the greater majority of Muslims; variations apply in some Muslim sects. These five pillars are:

Confessing the faith
Prayer
Fasting
Giving of alms
Pilgrimage to Mecca

Some Muslims add jihad as a sixth pillar.

All these are obligatory duties based on explicit injunctions in either the Quran or the *hadith*. There is no evading them. These aside, there are other duties that a good Muslim is expected to carry out, but while judged to be 'necessary' they are not, like the others, 'obligatory'.

Supreme importance is attached to these duties by most Muslims. They believe, on the authority of the Quran, that salvation is by 'works' such as these. Hence their concern, even anxiety and fear, to fulfil their duties. The representation of a pair of scales on the walls of Muslim buildings conveys to them more than the idea of justice. Those scales remind them of the statement in the Quran:

> Then those whose balance
> (Of good deeds) is heavy –
> They will attain salvation:
> But those whose balance
> Is light, will be those
> Who have lost their souls;
> In Hell they will abide. (Q 23:102, 103)

CONFESSING THE FAITH [*shahada*]

Shahada [confession] derives from an Arabic root that yields the meaning 'testify', so that, strictly speaking, a Muslim's confession of faith takes the form:

> 'I testify that there is no god but Allah and that Muhammad is the Apostle of Allah.'

PRAYER [*salah*]

1. Clothing

Clothing worn at a time of prayer is important to a Muslim, as the forehead must touch the ground. Muslim men wear brimless hats or turbans. In traditional clothing, the man normally removes his trousers under his long robes to pray and all Muslims remove their shoes.

2. Ablutions

Before a Muslim begins to pray, certain ceremonial ablutions must be performed. These are of three kinds.

(a) *wudu* – the lesser ablution. This is the most common form wherever water is available, and is customary before the appointed daily prayers.

Precise rules are prescribed for the washing of four parts of the body: the face, from the top of the forehead to the chin and as far as each ear; the hands and arms, up to the elbows; a quarter of the head is rubbed with the wet hand; and the feet are washed up to the ankles. Shias merely wipe – or rather rub – the feet. Many Muslims believe that, should any of these parts of the body be left unwashed, then the subsequent prayers, even if correctly recited, are robbed of all value.

In addition to the four main rules are fourteen minor ones. These include: to utter one of the names of Allah at the commencement of the ablutions; to clean one's teeth; to rinse out the mouth three times; to put water in the nostrils three times (the reason given for this particular injunction being a remark believed to have been made by Muhammad about those who wake up from sleep that 'Satan takes up his abode in the nose'); and to observe the proper order in washing the various parts of the head and body. The beard must be combed with wet fingers; one must rub under and between the toes with the wet fingers of the left hand, commencing with the toes of the right foot and finishing with the toes of the left foot.

It is an orthodox Muslim's confident belief, based on a saying attributed to Muhammad, that his little sins will be forgiven after such ablutions, duly followed by prayer.

(b) *ghusl* – the bathing of the entire body after certain legal defilements. In this case, water must be poured three times over the right shoulder, three times over the left, and finally, three times on the head. Besides this, there are three more 'obligatory' regulations: the mouth must be rinsed, water must be put in the nostrils, and the entire body must be washed. Not one hair should be left dry in the process.

(c) *tayammum* – purification by sand or earth. This procedure is prescribed to meet special circumstances; for instance, when water is not procurable within a distance of two miles, or when one is sick and the use of water might prove dangerous, or when water cannot be obtained without the risk of encountering an enemy, a wild beast or a reptile. It may be resorted to by someone who, delayed by some festival or funeral, has insufficient time for water ablutions. This cleansing is carried out by striking the sand or earth with one's open hands and then rubbing them over the face and arms up to the elbow.

3. The recitation of prayers

Having performed the necessary ablutions, the worshipper is now ready to recite the prescribed prayers. These may be said in private or in public, and it is a common sight to see Muslim men, singly or in ranks, saying their prayers in the street and other public places, if they happen to be there when the time is due. But prayers said along with a congregation in a mosque are judged to be more meritorious.

The face should be turned towards the *qibla* [direction of prayer] i.e. towards Mecca. There is a *mihrab*, or niche, in the wall of each mosque which indicates this direction.

4. *The call to prayer*

Prayer in a mosque is preceded by the *adhan* [call to prayer]. This call is chanted, in penetrating tones, by the muezzin from high up in a minaret of the mosque. It is common to use loudspeakers for amplification today. The call is made five times a day, and is composed of short sentences that elicit similarly worded 'responses', sentence by sentence, from worshippers within hearing who intend to say their prayers. The muezzin calls out: 'Allah is great. I confess that there is no god but Allah. I testify Muhammad is the Apostle of Allah. Come to prayer; come to do good.' Early in the morning he calls, 'Prayer is better than sleep. Allah is great. There is no god but Allah.'

5. *Postures in prayer*

During the course of the prayer, certain postures are assumed and genuflections made by the worshipper in accordance with detailed rules. The actual words of these prayers are a recitation, in Arabic, of some passages of the Quran, mainly the very short suras, placed in the canonical Quran at the close of the book, together with the *fatiha*, the name given to sura 1. To close the eyes during prayers would meet with the disapproval of the orthodox.

At prescribed intervals during such recitation, the worshipper utters the *takbir* [ascription of greatness to Allah], i.e. the well-known words, *Allahu Akbar* [Allah is great]. There immediately follows a lowly prostration, in a kneeling position, until the forehead actually touches the ground.

A certain number of set portions constitutes one complete recitation, and a worshipper may offer two or more such *rakaat* [units of prayer], according to whatever may have been his previously declared intention, said on hearing the call to prayer.

At the conclusion of these *rakaat* the worshipper offers the *durud*, or prayer for Muhammad which runs: 'O Allah, have mercy on Muhammad and on his descendants. Thou art to be praised and Thou art great', etc. He then turns his head, first to the right and repeats the *salam*, or salutation: 'The peace and mercy of Allah be with you', then to the left with the same words.

At the conclusion of the prayer, the hands are raised shoulder high, with palms upturned to heaven, and the worshipper offers up a final supplication, either in Arabic or using their customary language, and then draws the hands down over the face and on to the chest as if conveying the asked-for blessing to every part of the body.

6. *The times of prayer*

Tradition, not the Quran, has fixed the number of obligatory daily prayers as five. These are named and defined as follows:

> *fajr* – at dawn, before sunrise
> *zuhr* – soon after mid-day
> *asr* – mid-afternoon
> *maghrib* – soon after sunset
> *isha* – after nightfall.

The prayers on Friday [*jumma* – the Islamic holy day] take the place of the customary mid-day prayer. They differ in being preceded by an address (*khutba*) delivered by the imam [mosque leader].

7. *Voluntary petitions [dua]*

These are personal supplications to request help of various kinds according to the situation. They do not follow any set ritual or pattern.

FASTING [*sawm*]

Fasting is mainly practised during the daytimes of the ninth month, Ramadan. This is generally believed to commemorate the occasion when Muhammad received his initial revelation from the angel Gabriel. Fasting is defined as abstinence from food and drink, perfumes, tobacco, and sexual intercourse, between sunrise and sunset.

Each day, as soon as the sun has set, Muslims break their fast by the ritual act of eating a date or drinking water. A prayer is said: 'O Allah, I fasted for Thy sake and had faith in Thee, and confided in Thee, and now I break the fast with the food Thou givest. Accept this act.'

After that a large and delicious meal is eaten, called *iftar*.

It is an obligatory duty to fast during the month of Ramadan. Young children and the mentally disabled are excused, while the sick, those on a journey, pregnant women and nursing mothers may postpone it to another time. The aged and infirm must, in lieu of fasting, feed a poor person. There are other fasts also, but these are voluntary.

The fast of Ramadan begins with the first sighting of the new moon, marking the opening of the month, and is rigidly kept. In the heat of a tropical summer, or in the long summer days of the high latitudes, the

fast can be a severe trial. However, Muslim employers
do not usually expect much work from their employees
during Ramadan. As well as the exuberant feasting
each evening after sunset, there is a joyful celebration
at the end of the month (*id-ul-fitr*).

Certain acts render the fast invalid: if, when clean-
ing the teeth, a drop of water should pass down the
throat; if food is eaten under compulsion; if medicine
is put into the ear, nose, or even a wound in the head;
if a meal has been taken on the erroneous supposition
that it was night-time; if after the night meal a por-
tion of food larger than a grain of corn should remain
between the teeth or in a cavity of a tooth; if food is
vomited. In all such cases another day's fast must be
kept. Where the fast is wilfully broken, certain alternative penalties are prescribed. It used to be that the
delinquent had to atone by setting free a slave, or by
fasting every day for two months, or by giving sixty
persons two meals each, or one person twice-daily
meals for sixty days. Even now imprisonment and
fines are enforced in certain countries.

GIVING OF ALMS [*zakat*]

In Islam, two terms are used for almsgiving: *zakat*,
obligatory alms due – subject to certain conditions –
from every Muslim; and *sadaqa*, voluntary offerings,
made at the time of the annual festival known as
id-ul-fitr, at the end of Ramadan. This second term
may be used of alms in general.

It is an obligatory duty for every Muslim to give
zakat in proportion to their property, provided that they
have sufficient for subsistence. The conditions which

make *zakat* incumbent upon one are that a person should be free, sane, adult and a Muslim, and the possessor of the statutory amount of property. In Sunni Islam the rate is 2.5 per cent.

Zakat is to be given to certain classes of Muslim people, which include not only the poor and needy but also those in debt, travellers, those who administered the funds and recent converts to Islam. The donations could also be used for 'the cause of Allah', a phrase which encompasses jihad (Q 9:60). *Zakat*, from the beginning, could be given to a believing slave to enable him to purchase his freedom, or to enable a poor person to undertake the hajj. But *zakat* must not be used for the building of mosques, funeral expenses, or the liquidation of debts of a deceased person; neither is it permitted to give it to parents or grandparents, children or grandchildren. These prohibitions are often not observed today.

PILGRIMAGE TO MECCA [hajj]

This also is an obligatory duty, as commanded in the Quran:

> And proclaim the Pilgrimage
> Among men ...
> Then let them complete
> The rites prescribed
> For them, perform their vows,
> And (again) circumambulate
> The Ancient House. (Q 22:27-29)

Another passage concerning this 'house' i.e. the Kaaba, which is called 'the house of God', reads:

Pilgrimage thereto is a duty
Men owe to Allah, –
Those who can afford
The journey ... (Q 3:97)

A well-known commentator declared that the words
'can afford' were interpreted by Muhammad himself
to mean the possession of food for the journey and an
animal to ride on. Some traditions permit the sending
of a substitute, even posthumously.

Muhammad is said to have declared that it is necessary for a believer to make the pilgrimage only once
in his lifetime; any additional pilgrimages to the holy
city are 'voluntary'. If a child makes the pilgrimage he
must go again on coming of age. This pilgrimage must
be made in the twelfth month, Dhul hijjah.

The precincts of the Kaaba at Mecca are revered
as the supposed scene of Hagar's distress for her son
Ishmael. According to some legends Abraham and
Ishmael established the pilgrimage to Arafat, culmi-
nating with the sacrifice at Mina in remembrance of
the sacrifice made by Abraham.

There are very intricate rules laid down for the
performance of the pilgrimage, which vary between
different schools of Islamic law. Some parts are obligatory, others are merely 'necessary'. At the heart of the
rites is the ceremony of walking seven times round the
Kaaba. This seven-fold circumambulation is called
the *tawaf*. The pilgrims dress in white.

During the circumambulation of the Kaaba, the
pilgrim is expected to kiss the Black Stone. This is
the most venerated object in the ancient shrine. It is

probably a meteorite, and from of old has been treated with awe as something that fell from the sky. According to one tradition, Muhammad said: 'The Black Stone came down from paradise. It was whiter than milk, but the sins of the children of Adam have made it black [i.e. through kissing it].'

If the crowd is so large that the pilgrim cannot get near enough to kiss, he or she must touch it with the hand, or with a staff, and kiss that which has been in contact with the stone. At this time the pilgrim says, 'O Allah, I do this in Thy belief and in verification of Thy book and in pursuance of Thy prophet's example. May Allah bless and preserve him! O accept Thou my supplication, diminish my obstacles, pity my humiliation, and graciously grant me Thy pardon.'

Over a period of several days various other sacred places are visited in a certain order, including Mount Arafat and the valley of Mina. At Mina, stones are thrown at three pillars, one of which symbolises the devil. At the end animals are sacrificed, and the male pilgrim shaves his head. Henceforth he is known and respected as a 'hajji', one who has made the pilgrimage to Mecca.

Subsequently, most pilgrims make the *ziyara* or visit to the tomb of Muhammad at Medina.

The entire set of ceremonies connected with the hajj were taken over by Muhammad, possibly with very little change, from pre-Islamic paganism.

Five

Women in Islam

A WOMAN'S PLACE IN THE FAMILY

Muslim women are always under the protection of a male relative: father, husband, brother, uncle or son. Many of the restrictions on a woman are due to the need for her honour – on which the honour of the whole family depends – to be carefully preserved. It will be argued that the more strictly she is controlled the more highly she is valued. It is essential for a girl to be a virgin at marriage.

A woman will often need permission from a male relative even to visit her mother or sisters. She will seldom go out alone, but usually with a close male relative or a number of female relatives. Even young children can chaperone their mothers or elder sisters in this way.

The woman's place is in the home. Her role is to produce sons for her husband, to care for them, and to do the housework. Some women may go out to work to add to the family's finances, but this is usually only in cases of necessity. The husband will rarely assist with the housework, even if his wife has a full-time job. Although the wife normally does the cooking, in some societies the husband will cook for special occasions.

When mixed groups are visiting, the women of the family will often stay in an inner room while the men entertain the male visitors and the less well-known female visitors. A female Christian visitor may often find herself put in this mixed-sex room, away from the women of the family. To be invited to join the women in the inner family room is a compliment that indicates intimacy and trust.

CLOTHING

Islam teaches that a woman must dress modestly, covering herself from neck to wrist and ankle as well as covering her hair. Different cultures fulfil these criteria in different ways. The covering should be opaque and loose-fitting. Long, loose hair is considered immodest.

In some parts of the world, further demands are placed by custom on the woman, for example, covering the feet, hands or face. In some cultures, though brightly-coloured clothes may be worn in the home, these must be covered with a dark outer garment when going out.

The *hijab* – the woman's veil and head-covering – can have political significance. In some more secular countries, such as Turkey, it is banned in certain contexts such as schools, universities and government offices. In conservative countries, such as Saudi Arabia, it is obligatory. In the West it can be a point of controversy where Muslim girls may be disallowed from wearing it to school, or Muslim women forbidden to wear it at work. Many young Muslim women have adopted the *hijab* in recent years both in the West and elsewhere. Sometimes it is because of family pressure but sometimes by their own choice through religious conviction.

MARRIAGE

Marriage is seen in the Quran as a gift from God (Q 16:72) and the normal human condition (Q 4:25). Singleness is viewed as very undesirable and probably an indication of immorality. Likewise voluntary childlessness is a completely baffling concept to most Muslims. There are, however, a few sections of Muslim society where celibacy for religious reasons is approved.

Marriage is not so much a joining of the two individuals involved as a joining of their respective families. As such, marriages are almost always arranged by the families concerned, with little or no consultation with the young couple, who sometimes do not even see each other until the wedding day. Strictly speaking, the young person is allowed to refuse the prospective marriage partner whom their family chooses for them, but in practice there is often enormous pressure and emotional blackmail put on them to accept and not disgrace their family by refusing. The bride is not necessarily even present at the marriage contract ceremony, but can be represented by a male relative.

It is common in some societies for marriages to be arranged with close relatives, for example, first and second cousins. If the marriage is arranged outside the family, then factors such as financial situation and social status are very important in making the choice. A Muslim man is permitted to marry a Christian or

Jewish woman, but a Muslim woman can marry only a Muslim man.

Love is expected to grow between husband and wife after their marriage, rather than before. Even so, this love is not usually expected to blossom into the kind of devotion and tender companionship that Westerners generally hope for in marriage. A Muslim girl is taught from childhood to look to her children, especially her sons, for love rather than to her husband, who is primarily the provider and protector. Generally the closest bond in a Muslim family is between mother and son.

For young Muslims who have grown up in a Western society there can be a very painful conflict between the ideals of the older generations in their families and the ideals of the majority culture. It is common in Britain for a spouse to be found and brought over from the 'home country', so that husband and wife almost inevitably come to the marriage with radically different expectations.

However, many Muslim families in the West nowadays relax the rules somewhat. For example, they may allow the young couple to spend a few hours talking together before they must decide whether to get married. The happiest young couples are probably those whose 'love match' is approved by their respective families, who will then take over, make the usual arrangements and conduct the normal negotiations with each other.

Although both families and the groom will rejoice over the coming marriage, the bride is not necessarily expected to do so in a traditionally arranged marriage. She will be leaving her family to live with a strange family she does not know. A smiling bride is considered improper in some societies, and tears (of sadness, not joy) are required to show how much she will miss her family.

It is a terrible disgrace for an unhappy wife to leave her husband. Her own family – who would share her disgrace – will do all they can to prevent her returning to them, no matter how badly she is being treated by her husband or in-laws.

A Muslim man is permitted to have up to four wives at the same time, though he is required to treat them all equally. He is also permitted to beat a disobedient wife (Q 4:34).

DIVORCE

According to sharia, it is easy for a Muslim man to divorce his wife; he need only say to her three times in front of witnesses: 'I divorce you.' On the other hand, it is very difficult for a woman to divorce her husband.

The children of a marriage belong to the husband and his family. Whether the wife is divorced or widowed, she must hand over the children (though she can keep babies until she has finished breast-feeding them, which is supposed to be at the age of two).

In Shia Islam there is the possibility of temporary marriages called *muta*. The length of the marriage is agreed in the marriage contract, and can vary from one hour to ninety-nine years. Given that men can have more than one wife simultaneously, in effect this arrangement can amount to legalised prostitution.

FAMILY PLANNING AND ABORTION

Although large families are generally sought after, contraception is not forbidden in Islam. Abortion is permitted, although some scholars allow it only if the mother's life is in danger or if there is a strong possibility that the baby will be severely disabled. The unborn baby must be no more than 40 to 120 days old, the exact figure depending on which school of sharia is followed.

Because all the children of a Muslim man are considered Muslims, whatever the religion of the mother, deliberately fathering many Muslim children has been one of the ways in which Islam has been spread at certain times and places. This mindset is apparently behind the widespread rape of Christian women by Muslim men that happens today in some Muslim countries. It should be noted that rape is also considered to dishonour the woman. A Muslim mission strategy being used in certain parts of Africa is for Muslim men to marry Christian women, and some are paid for each Christian woman they manage to marry, more if a woman is a pastor's daughter.

SPIRITUAL DUTIES

Women are required to practise the five pillars of Islam, as men are, though menstruation is considered to invalidate prayer and fasting. Muslim societies vary as to whether women are expected to attend public prayers in the mosque. Even if they are, they will do so in a secluded place, separate from and invisible to the men. They are promised the same heavenly reward (Q 16:97) though it has to be said that a paradise full of beautiful virgins (Q 44:54; 55:72) would not seem to be as great a delight for women as for men. Several *ahadith* state that a woman's obedience to her husband is the main prerequisite for her to get to heaven.

Many women have little knowledge of true Islam or the teachings of the Quran, though they generally know all about the day of judgment. Often they are familiar with certain *ahadith* indicating that most women will go to hell (though most men will go to heaven). It is hardly surprising that their lives are often dominated by superstition and fear, and many practise 'folk Islam' (see pp. 107-8).

LEGAL STATUS

The sharia gives women only half the value of men in terms of testimony and compensation. Thus two female witnesses equal one male witness in an Islamic law court (where verdicts are arrived at primarily by counting the number of witnesses on each side). The same injury sustained by a man and by a woman will result in compensation for the woman at 50 per cent of what the man receives. Similarly, a daughter generally inherits only half what her brother does; this is justified by the greater financial responsibilities of men.

The unequal position of women as regards divorce and polygamy has already been mentioned.

Six

Islamic history
(See also Appendix II)

THE RIGHTLY GUIDED CALIPHS AND THE EXPANSION OF ISLAM

Muhammad was succeeded as caliph (leader of the Muslim community) in 632 by Abu Bakr, one of his earliest followers. Abu Bakr not only put down a number of rebellions that sprang up as soon as Muhammad had died, thus strengthening and stabilising the Islamic state, but also began hostilities against the Byzantine and Persian empires. In his short reign Syria was conquered by the Islamic armies.

Abu Bakr was succeeded in 634 by Caliph Umar, who was assassinated in 644 and succeeded by Caliph Uthman. During this time Iraq, Persia and Egypt fell in quick succession, and by 656 (when Uthman was assassinated) the boundaries of Islam had reached Afghanistan in the east, Libya in the west and the Caucasus mountains in the north.

The reign of the fourth caliph, Caliph Ali (656-661; Ali ibn Abu Talib, the husband of Muhammad's daughter Fatima), saw a huge and violent three-way split within the Muslim community over the issue of who was eligible to be caliph (see p. 103). It was at this point that Shia Islam originated. After five years of civil war, Ali was assassinated and Muawiyya (head of Uthman's clan, the Umayyads) was established as caliph with his capital in Damascus. Ali's death marked the end of an era which Muslims look back on as a Golden Age, the age of the four Rightly Guided (*Rashidun*) Caliphs, each of whom had had a close personal connection to Muhammad.

SUNNI EMPIRES

From the reign of Muawiyya (661-680) onward, the caliphate became hereditary, and a series of powerful Sunni dynasties ruled most of the Muslim world. The conquest and conversion of non-Muslim lands continued rapidly.

Reasons for such a rapid expansion are not hard to find. The Arab peoples, for so long divided along tribal lines, had been united under the dynamic leadership of Muhammad and continued to be driven by religious zeal and a desire for plunder. Many Christians living under the Byzantine Empire hated its rule and did not want to defend it.

The once vigorous Church in North Africa, which had known the leadership of such men as Augustine, Athanasius, Cyprian and Tertullian, was by this time troubled by division and power struggles. Although it survived the initial Muslim conquest in the seventh century, it grew gradually weaker in the years of Muslim rule. Under the puritanical Almohads (1094-1163) the Church was finally eliminated, except in Egypt, where a large Coptic community survived.

The Umayyads (661-750)

The Umayyads ruled from Damascus and continued
the fight against Byzantium and the drive into North
Africa, crossing into Spain (711), and their advance
into France was halted only by the battle of Tours/
Poitiers in 732. The expansion eastward into Central
Asia and north India was also pursued, and Muslim
armies reached Multan in the Punjab in 713.

The Abbasids (750-1258)

In 750 the Umayyads were replaced in a bloody revolt
by the Abbasids, a dynasty descended from an uncle of
Muhammad named Abbas. They had developed their
major power base in Persia, supported by non-Arab
Muslims who resented Arab superiority. It was during
the time of the early Abbasids that the detailed sharia
regulations were developed by religious scholars.
Sufism [Islamic mysticism] also developed under the
Abbasids, as did a group known as the Mutazilites,
who held that the Quran was created for the time and
place when Muhammad received it, rather than existing eternally in heaven.

Abbasid rule, based on their new capital of Baghdad, brought in another 'golden age' of classical Islam
in the ninth and tenth centuries, which included
a great flowering of the sciences and arts. Christian
and Jewish minorities played an important part in this
cultural flourishing, as did the translation of ancient
Greek works.

Gradually the power of the caliphs decreased as
various provinces became largely independent under
strong local Muslim rulers. In 1258 Baghdad was

conquered, and although the Abbasid caliphate was
later revived in Cairo the caliph was thereafter just
a figurehead without real power.

The Seljuks (mid 11ᵗʰ century to mid 13ᵗʰ century)
From the tenth century onwards the Seljuks, a nomadic
Turkic tribal grouping from Central Asia, moved
westwards into Persia, Azerbaijan and Anatolia. Many
of their tribes converted to Sunni Islam. The Turks
formed a new military class and became front-line
soldiers of the Muslim expansion into the Christian
Byzantine Empire. Turkic slave soldiers (Mamelukes,
literally 'owned') were increasingly used to strengthen
the Islamic Empire's armies, and their commanders
(sultans) became powerful political players.

In due course the Seljuks abandoned their dependent relationship with Islam and took real power. The
'Greater' Seljuks conquered the Muslim heartlands in
Persia and Baghdad between about 1035 and 1055.
At the same time another group of Seljuks, known as
the 'Lesser' Seljuks, were active in Anatolia against
the Byzantine Empire.

During the Crusades the Mameluke Egyptian
sultans played a major role in defeating the Crusader
armies and re-establishing Muslim rule in the areas
once held by them.

In the late twelfth and early thirteenth centuries
the power of the Greater Seljuks declined because of
internal dynastic divisions and external attack from
the Mongols (see below). The Lesser Seljuks in Anatolia kept their power a little longer but were defeated
by the Mongols in 1243, although they continued to
govern Anatolia until the early fourteenth century.

The Ayyubids (1171-1250)

Saladin (Salah al-Din), son of a Kurdish general named Ayyoub, brought down the Ismaili Shia Fatimid Empire in 1171 and established the Ayyubid dynasty, which ruled both Egypt and Syria. After many famous exploits against the Crusaders, he died in 1193, and others of the dynasty ruled until 1250, when the last Ayyubid sultan was removed in a coup by a Mameluke commander.

The Mamelukes (1250-1517)

The Mamelukes had been slave soldiers introduced by the Abbasids as a professional army to replace the unreliable Arab tribal forces. The Mameluke state set up in Egypt (1250-1517) also governed south-eastern Asia Minor, Syria and western Arabia. To increase their legitimacy they installed a puppet Abbasid caliph in Cairo under their complete control. Until the mid-fifteenth century, the Mameluke state was the undisputed military power of the western Muslim world. Their control over Mecca and Medina gave them additional legitimacy in Muslim eyes.

The Mongols

Following the rise of Genghis Khan as the ruler of all the Mongols, his armies invaded Muslim areas in Central Asia and Iran and destroyed Baghdad in 1258, ending the Abbasid caliphate. The Mongols were halted in Syria by an Egyptian Mameluke army in 1260, but set up Mongol states in the vast areas they had conquered, which later converted to Sunni Islam. In the fourteenth century Timurlane (ruled

1370-1405) created a vast empire with its capital in Samarkand. He crushed the last vestiges of Christianity in Central Asia.

SHIA EMPIRES

(see p. 103-5 for the origins and beliefs of Shia Islam)

The Shia initially supported the Abbasids, hoping they would give the caliphate to a descendant of Caliph Ali. But the Abbasids gradually became more firmly committed to Sunni Islam, and the Shia were sidelined. During the Abbasid period the main theological position of Twelver Shia Islam was developed, and the line of accepted imams was established; many of them had to live in hiding for fear of the Abbasid authorities. From 954 to 1055 the Shia enjoyed a period of greater freedom while the Shia Buyid dynasty held power in Baghdad, but this came to an end when the Sunni Seljuks rose to power.

Meanwhile, a local Shia dynasty, the Hamdanids, emerged in Syria, ruling Aleppo and Mosul under nominal Abbasid rule from 935 to 1016.

The Turkoman Safavid dynasty controlled Persia from 1501 under Shah Ismail. He accepted Twelver Shiism as the state religion and forced the Sunni population to convert to his creed. (See p. 99 for the later history of the Safavid Empire.)

The Fatimids (910-1171)

An Ismaili caliphate rivalling the Sunni one was established in Ifriqiya (modern-day Libya and Tunisia) in 910 by the Fatimids. They were a dynasty claiming to be descended from Muhammad's daughter,

Fatima. The first three Fatimid caliphs ruled only in Ifriqiya, but they claimed the right to be leaders of the whole Muslim world. In 969 Mu'izz, the fourth Fatimid caliph, conquered Egypt and founded the new city of Cairo as his capital and the great mosque of al-Azhar as the religious centre of Ismailism. From it the Ismaili faith was propagated in all directions.

The Fatimids ruled Egypt for two centuries and competed with the Abbasids of Baghdad for control of the entire Muslim world. They rapidly expanded their empire over Syria, Palestine and Arabia, including the holy cities of Mecca and Medina. They were great patrons of culture and art, and under them Egypt became the centre of a flourishing civilisation. In the twelfth century the power of the caliphs declined as they became mere figureheads while their *wazirs* ruled in their name.

The Sunni Ayyubid sultan, Saladin, abolished the Fatimid caliphate in 1171.

The Nizari Ismailis (Assassins)

The Nizari branch of Ismaili Islam created a small Ismaili state based at the fortress of Alamut in the mountains of northern Persia. There were also Nizari Ismailis in Syria; their most famous leader, Rashid al-Din Sinan (1133-1193), was known as 'The Old Man of the Mountain'. They used assassination as a political weapon against both Muslim and Christian leaders, and generally performed it very openly to create maximum publicity and fear. Because of their hatred for the Sunnis, the Assassins were willing to ally themselves for short periods with the Crusaders.

The Ismailis in turn were hated by the Sunnis, and sporadic massacres of Ismailis were common. Alamut fell to the Mongols in 1256, and at the same time the Mamelukes stamped out Ismaili power in Syria. The last Assassin Imam smuggled his son to Azerbaijan, and the movement later spread to the Indian subcontinent. In 1840 Imam Hassan Ali Shah, who had taken the title of Agha Khan, settled in India. There are small communities of Nizari Ismailis today, mainly in India, Pakistan, Afghanistan, East Africa, Syria and the West.

THE CRUSADES

The conquest of the Holy Land and other Christian territories such as Syria, Egypt, North Africa and Spain by Muslim armies in the initial Islamic jihad of the seventh century was deeply mourned across the Christian world. The Crusades, which were a delayed Christian reaction to this jihad, began at the request of the Byzantine Emperor and of Christians in the Middle East, who pleaded with their fellow-Christians in Europe for assistance against their Muslim oppressors and attackers. Under Fatimid rule in Egypt there was sporadic persecution of Christians, especially under Caliph al-Hakim (985-1021), who in 1009 demolished the Church of the Holy Sepulchre in Jerusalem and prohibited Christians from visiting the site for eleven years. Furthermore, the Byzantine Empire was under attack by the Seljuk Turks, who also disrupted Christian pilgrimage to the Christian holy sites in Jerusalem.

The first Crusade set off in 1096, and eight further crusades followed over the next 200 years. Both Muslims and Crusaders fought cruelly. After initial Crusader success, Christian states were set up in Syria and Palestine. For a while they became part of the local scene, engaging in sporadic alliances with some Muslim states against other Christian and Muslim states. Gradually, however, the tide turned against the Crusaders, and Sultan Saladin achieved a notable military success when he retook Jerusalem for Islam in 1187. The Mamelukes of Egypt continued the assault on the Crusader kingdoms, and the last Crusader castle fell in 1291.

Muslims today have used the Crusades to extract admissions of guilt from modern Westerners who are uneasy about imperialism, colonialism and cultural insensitivity. It must be admitted that after the first Crusade the motives and behaviour of the Christians deteriorated, and they even killed Jews and eastern Christians. But in this debate the vital fact that the Crusades were a counterattack in response to Muslim jihad and ill-treatment of Christians is rarely mentioned.

ISLAMIC SPAIN – AL-ANDALUS (711-1492)

The Muslim conquest of Christian Spain began in 711 under the Berber general Tariq Ibn Ziyad, who brought most of the Iberian Peninsula under Islamic rule in a seven-year campaign. The Muslims then moved northeast across the Pyrenees but were defeated by the Frankish leader Charles Martel at the Battle of Tours/ Poitiers in 732. Christians in the northern enclaves that escaped Muslim rule began a long process of resistance and reconquest (*Reconquista*), which lasted almost 800 years.

Al-Andalus was at first ruled by governors appointed by the Umayyad caliph in Damascus. When the Umayyads fell to the Abbasids in 750, the Umayyad Prince Abd al-Rahman escaped the massacre of his family. He reached Spain in 756, where he established himself as the Emir of Cordoba, and refused to submit to the distant new Abbasid caliph. In 929 his grandson, Abd al-Rahman III, proclaimed himself caliph in Cordoba, thus competing in prestige with the Abbasid caliphs in Baghdad and with the Fatimid caliphs in Tunisia and Egypt.

The caliphate (929-1031) was the golden age of Al-Andalus. Cordoba had a population of some 100,000 and was larger and more prosperous than any other city in Europe (except for Constantinople). It was one of the most important cultural centres of the Muslim world, and its philosophers and scholars had a significant influence on the intellectual life of medieval Europe.

The Umayyads were inconsistent in their treatment of non-Muslims in Al-Andalus. There was a period of tolerance beginning in 912, with the reign of Abd al-Rahman III and his son, Al-Hakam II, in which the Jews and Christians of Al-Andalus prospered. But with the death of Al-Hakam III in 976, the situation of Jews and Christians deteriorated.

In 1031 the last Umayyad caliph was expelled from Cordoba, and the caliphate began to disintegrate into a number of small independent states (*taifas*), too weak to defend themselves against raids from the Christian states in the north. In December 1066 the Jews were expelled from Granada and 1,500 Jewish families who refused to leave were killed.

The *taifa* states requested help from the puritanical Almoravid rulers of North Africa, who arrived in 1086 and took the opportunity to conquer the *taifa* kingdoms themselves and create a reunified Islamic state in Spain. The Almoravids and their more fanatical Almohad successors were much less tolerant than the Umayyads and persecuted Christians and Jews. Under the Almoravids Jews were forced to convert to Islam, and Christians were expelled, many to North Africa. After the Almohads had defeated the Almoravids in 1148 and taken power, Jews were again forced to convert to Islam; the conquerors confiscated their property and sold many into slavery. Christians were also severely persecuted and on occasion expelled.

In 1212 a Christian coalition under the Castilian king Alfonso VIII decisively defeated the Almohads at the Battle of Las Navas de Tolosa. This was the beginning of the end of Muslim dominance in Spain, and the Muslims were gradually driven south until only Granada remained under Muslim control. Granada survived for nearly three more centuries as a vassal state of Castile. In 1492, Boabdil, the last Emir of Granada, surrendered to armies of Christian Spain, united under Isabella I of Castile and Ferdinand II of Aragon.

THE PRE-MODERN AGE

By the seventeenth century three large Muslim empires dominated the Muslim world: the Ottoman Empire (Sunni) in Asia Minor, the Middle East, North Africa and Europe; the Safavid Empire (Shia) in the Iranian heartland, parts of Central Asia and the Caucasus; and the Mughal Empire (Sunni) in northern India.

The Ottoman Empire

The Ottomans were a Turkish dynasty who had united all Turkish states in Asia Minor and in 1453 had captured Constantinople (renaming it Istanbul), thus bringing an end to the Christian Byzantine Empire. They then pushed into southern Europe, conquering most of the Balkans and twice reaching the gates of Vienna (1529 and 1683). Their best troops, the Janissaries, consisted of Christian boys from the Balkans forcibly taken from their families, converted to Islam and trained as professional soldiers. For hundreds of years Christian Europe lived in fear of the powerful, Muslim, Ottoman Empire and its gradual expansion into the European heartlands. The Ottomans also conquered the Mameluke Empire (which included Egypt, Syria, Palestine and the Arabian Peninsula), and were recognised as overlords by North African rulers as far west as Algeria. But as the empire weakened in later centuries, it lost lands to the Russian and Austrian Empires. It was finally dismantled by the Allies following the First World War.

The Safavid Empire (1501-1736)

Shah Ismail, who established the Shia Safavid Empire in Persia, claimed to be descended from Ali and Fatima. The Safavids based their legitimacy on their claims to be descendants of the Shia imams, representatives of the Hidden Imam and rulers until his return. Shah Ismail encouraged messianic expectations and established Twelver Shia Islam as the state religion in an effort to unite his empire against the Sunni Ottomans. Shia Islam was used to strengthen Safavid rule over the ethnically diverse population, and Shia religious scholars (*ulama*) became part of the state bureaucracy.

For two centuries there was warfare between the Safavid Empire and the Ottoman Empire until the border between them was stabilised. This left some large Shia populations under Ottoman rule and therefore vulnerable to Sunni persecution.

The Safavids later moved their capital from Tabriz to Isfahan, which was transformed into a magnificent city in which Persian culture and arts flourished.

The Mughal Empire (1526-1858)

This was founded in 1526 by Babur, a descendant of Genghis Khan and Timurlane. The early Mughal emperors made the empire larger and stronger until it covered most of India except for the far south. The Mughal Empire experienced a flourishing of arts and culture, and most Mughal rulers were fairly tolerant towards their non-Muslim subjects, seeing them as essential to the stability, economy and power of the empire. Under Aurangzeb (1658-1707), however, non-Muslims were replaced by Muslims in public offices, and *dhimmi* status was harshly enforced. Aurangzeb's continual wars of expansion weakened his empire, and after his death its power rapidly waned. The British stepped into the power vacuum and in effect became masters of the Muslim state. They finally deposed its last emperor in 1858 and added the territory to their other Indian possessions.

Expansion into South-East Asia

Islam spread from various parts of Arabia and India to the Malay peninsula and to the Indonesian archipelago during the twelfth to fifteenth centuries. At the same time Islam also reached the coastlines of what are now Burma (Myanmar) and Thailand.

The establishing of Islam in south-east Asia differed from that in most other regions: it was not imposed by military conquest but brought by traders and Sufis. The existing ruling regimes were not overthrown but were converted to Islam, and then gradually the rest of the population followed suit.

A special element of south-east Asian Islam is its close link to the Malay people, who are spread from southern Thailand to the southern Philippines, crossing the boundaries of modern nation-states. Islam in south-east Asia tended to fuse with the pre-Islamic (mainly Hindu) religion. It is now taking a stricter form through the influence of Wahhabi/Salafi Islam from Saudi Arabia.

Expansion into Sub-Saharan Africa

The Arabs had rapidly conquered North Africa in the first wave of Islamic expansion, which set in motion a twofold process of Islamisation and Arabisation of the local Berber population. Islam expanded into sub-Saharan Africa from two directions: from the north into the Sahel, brought by Berber conquerors and traders along the Sahara caravan routes; and along the East African coastline, brought by Muslim Arab traders and conquerors arriving by sea from Arabia. There was also migration and settlement, particularly in East Africa, and Muslim missionary work, especially by Sufis.

The expansion of Islam south of Egypt was blocked for a while by the three Nubian Christian kingdoms that flourished along the Nile for some 600 years, but they finally fell between the fourteenth and sixteenth centuries, opening the way for further Muslim expansion.

Islam arrived in South Africa mainly through Muslim Malay slaves and Muslim Indian labourers in the eighteenth and nineteenth centuries.

European Colonialism

While Muslim states were dominant in world politics for the first thousand years following the founding of Islam, Muslim countries have been on the defensive for the last three hundred years since the rise of European colonialism. The eighteenth and nineteenth centuries saw most of the Muslim world forced to yield to European powers. This process reached its climax with the fall of the Ottoman Empire after the First World War. Various resistance movements that proclaimed jihad against the Western powers were put down by superior forces.

For Muslims accustomed to seeing political power as their God-given right, this was a shocking, unnerving

and humiliating experience. It gave rise to various
movements of reform and resistance as Muslims
searched for the reason for their unaccustomed
weakness. (See pp. 109-11 on radical Islam.)

THE ERA OF INDEPENDENCE

The majority of Muslim states had gained their
independence by 1965. Many experimented with
socialism. When this failed they then turned
increasingly to Islam. Most have failed to establish
stable democratic regimes or economic development
in line with their expanding populations. Many
Muslims blame this on what they see as Western neo-
colonialism, which they believe is seeking to keep
Muslim states dependent on the West economically,
politically and culturally. Globalisation and Christian
missionary work are also seen by many Muslims as
part of Western efforts to dominate and weaken the
world of Islam.

Exceptions to the general rule are the oil-rich
Muslim states, such as Saudi Arabia and the Gulf
States, which have achieved enormous economic
power and wealth since the 1970s. This wealth has
been used to fund the resurgence of Islam worldwide
in its puritanical, anti-Western, Wahhabi/Salafi and
Islamist forms.

Seven

Diversity in Islam

SUNNI AND SHIA

Islam has two main divisions: Sunni and Shia. Sunni Muslims form the majority (about 90 per cent), and this book has mainly described Sunni beliefs and practices. Shia Muslims are a majority only in Iran, Iraq, Azerbaijan and Bahrain. In some places they are persecuted by Sunnis.

The split into Sunni and Shia originated little more than twenty years after Muhammad's death in a dispute over the succession to leadership of the Muslim community. The fourth caliph, who succeeded in 656, was Ali, the husband of Muhammad's daughter Fatima. He was not universally accepted as the rightful successor, and Muslims began to fight each other over this issue. Ali was eventually murdered in 661, and the struggle was continued by his two sons, Hassan and Hussain. Hassan was poisoned in about 670, and Hussain died at the Battle of Karbala in 680. Ali's followers, Shia Ali [the party of Ali], became the Shia Muslims.

Shia doctrines and practices
Shias hold that Ali was the first legitimate imam (their preferred word for 'caliph') and reject the first three.

They greatly revere him and his sons, their main annual festival being a commemoration of the martyrdom
of Hussain on 10th Muharram. This day is marked with
passion plays, wailing and flagellation. Shias believe
that only Ali's descendants, who through Fatima are
also descendants of Muhammad, can be imams. They
consider these imams to be infallible and sinless.

Shias add two more key beliefs to the six Muslim
articles of faith: the importance of the imamate and
that justice is part of God's nature. Their practice of
temporary marriages has already been mentioned.
Shias hold that *ijtihad* (logical deduction) may still be
practised, i.e. that parts of the sharia can be adapted.
By contrast most Sunnis believe that the sharia can
never be changed.

Perhaps the most important feature of Shia Islam
of which a Christian who is building a friendship
with a Shia Muslim should be aware is the practice
of *taqiyya* [dissimulation]. Shia Islam allows its followers to lie and deceive and deny what they really
believe, so long as they continue to adhere to their own
belief in their hearts. The tenth century Shia divine,
Ibn Babuya al-Saquq, stated, 'Our belief concerning
taqiyya is that it is obligatory ... God has described
the showing of friendship to unbelievers' as being
possible only 'in the state of *taqiyya*'. (See pp. 25-6
for more details on *taqiyya*.)

Sub-divisions of Shia Islam
Shias have split into many different sects. Amongst
the most well known are the Ismailis, led by the Agha
Khan. Both the Druzes and the Bahais also originated

from Shia Islam, though they have diverged so far from it that they are no longer considered to be Muslims.

The largest sub-division of Shias is called the 'Twelvers'. They acknowledge twelve imams, the first being Ali and the twelfth being Muhammad al-Mahdi, a four-year-old boy who disappeared into a cave near Baghdad in 873 or 874. The twelfth imam, called 'the hidden imam', is believed to be still alive and exerting a spiritual influence on his followers. In the last days he will return as the Mahdi [rightly guided one] and establish Islamic rule throughout the world.

The sixth imam, Jafar al-Sadiq (died 765), was especially important in the development and consolidation of the Shia theological and legal systems, and the Twelver Shia are often called Jafaris.

After the death of the sixth imam, his followers split over which of his two sons – Ismail or Musa – was the appointed successor. The followers of Ismail became known as Seveners or Ismailis. During the late eighth and early ninth centuries Ismail's descendants organised into an intricate, hierarchical, secret society. By the early tenth century there was growing discontent among the peasants, slaves and ordinary townsfolk of the Abbasid Empire, and Ismaili revolutionary propaganda appealed to all the resentful elements of society.

SUFISM – ISLAMIC MYSTICISM

The Sufis are the mystics of Islam. Sufism attracts followers from a wide range of intellectual and social backgrounds, who can belong to almost any group or sect of Islam except (probably) the Wahhabis and

Ahmadis. The founders of the various Sufi brotherhoods or orders are venerated as saints (*pirs*), as are
their successors. Saints are believed to have important powers of intercession and blessing. Al Ghazali
(1058-1111), the famous Persian theologian and
renewer of the Islamic faith, was a Sufi.

The movement began with ascetics who sought
to escape the world and live in austere simplicity,
calm and passivity. Poverty and purity were their
hallmarks. One ascetic in the eighth century took to
wearing a woollen robe, and this may be the origin
of the name 'Sufi', from the Arabic word for 'wool'.
Alternatively, the name could be derived from *safu*,
the Arabic for 'purity'.

Central to Sufism is the desire for a personal loving relationship with Allah and a feeling of closeness
to him, resulting ultimately in union with Allah. This
longing is expressed in many beautiful love poems.
The methods used to try to achieve such union include
meditation, contemplation and the tireless repetition of
one or another of Allah's names. This repetition is called
dhikr [remembering God], and its purpose is to induce
a trance. The Muslim rosary [*tasbih*] is also used. One of
the Sufi brotherhoods, the Maulawiya, who originated in
Turkey, use a rapid rotating dance to enter into a trance
and are sometimes called the 'whirling dervishes'.

Sufism has often been controversial. Even in the
early days Sufis were condemned by many Muslims
because their practices and even their clothes seemed
to have been derived from Christian hermits and monks
of the time. The fact that they also abandoned certain
Islamic prohibitions from time to time, for example,

drinking alcohol, also brought them condemnation from some orthodox Muslims.

Among Sufis the distinction between male and female tends to disappear. Some women even became revered saints and religious leaders. Many women follow Sufi saints today. Some become disciples of a chosen spiritual leader, though proper initiation is generally reserved for men. Many women go with their menfolk on pilgrimages to shrines of saints, particularly to celebrate the birth or the death of the saint and to secure his help with health and family problems.

The Sufis were and still are great missionaries. They were particularly active in Central Asia; for example, they brought Islam to the Mongols. Nowadays Sufism is an attractive option for Western converts to Islam. Sufis are not pacifists and have been instrumental in several jihad movements.

FOLK ISLAM

Folk Islam is one of the names given to a form of Islam practised by millions of ordinary Muslims as well as by many educated Muslims. This popular Islam is very different from the official version and is characterised by fear of evil powers, such as jinn and the evil eye, and the use of the occult. It is linked to Sufism and incorporates local pre-Islamic beliefs and superstitions into Islam.

Folk Islam is dominated by fear. It includes witchcraft, sorcery, spells, charms and curses, all designed to achieve certain aims. Talismans and amulets, for protection against evil spirits, are tied to clothing, tucked above doors or hung from rear-view car mirrors. The intercession of Muslim saints – living and dead – is also important. Ordinary Muslims visit local religious leaders or fortune-tellers to seek help with health problems, love troubles, demon-possession and many other difficulties.

The beliefs and practices of 'high Islam' – the Islam described earlier in this book – are given a different twist in 'low' Islam. Belief in the oneness of Allah becomes a set of magic formulae to use his names for personal advantage, such as obtaining healing or finding lost property. Belief in angels is expressed in a further doctrine of an individual's having a familiar spirit, a double of the opposite sex, born at the same time but the progeny of Satan. Belief in Allah's sacred books becomes belief in the power of the Quran as a fetish: certain chapters are useful against evil spirits; one particular verse is good for curing headaches; etc.

Likewise the pillars of Islam are transformed with extra layers of meaning in folk Islam. The words of the creed are seen as a supernatural means of fending off evil, and therefore appear on many amulets. The ablutions that precede prayer are believed to wash away demonic influence. Alms-giving wards off the evil eye of jealousy. Fasting and pilgrimage help to drive out evil spirits, banish sickness etc.

TRADITIONAL ISLAM

The majority of devout Muslims are traditionalists who accept Islam as it developed in the early centuries. They believe that sharia, as formulated in medieval times, can never be changed because 'the gates of independent reasoning' were closed after the various schools of law had been established. Traditionalists approach Islam through the four defined schools of law and the lengthy commentaries explaining them that were written by later scholars. Nevertheless many traditionalists are also involved in Sufism and folk Islam. Most reject any innovation, new interpretations or reformation and also reject secularism and Western culture.

RADICAL ISLAM

The last half century has seen the development of a form of Islam that is perhaps best called 'fundamentalist' or 'radical'. Its intention is to return to the origins of Islam. Muslims themselves often describe this process as 'reform', but non-Muslims must realise that the reform is not towards a liberal and modern stance but in the opposite direction.

Various arguments have been put forward as to why radical Islam has developed. One trigger appears to have been a reaction against colonialism. Another was the granting of independence to almost all the former colonies of the European powers, which gave greater confidence to previously subject Muslim peoples. (See p. 102.) Yet another was the start of the fifteenth century A.H. in November 1979 A.D.; it is held that Islam will be renewed at the turn of every century. Certainly the latter half of 1979 saw a number of dramatic Muslim actions, including the Iranian Revolution.

According to Islamic teaching, the only possible reason for Muslims to be defeated or humiliated is that they have not been faithful enough in practising their religion. Hence the drive for a purification and renewal of the Islamic faith by a return to the model of Muhammad and the first Islamic state in Medina. This model includes rule by sharia and expansion by jihad. Radicals yearn to recreate a golden age such as Islam experienced under the first four caliphs and under the various Muslim empires at the height of their military and cultural glory. The result is a movement to create a worldwide Islamic state under sharia.

Several theological themes are characteristic of the radical Islamic renewal movements. One is an emphasis on submitting unquestioningly to the authority of the Quran and *sunna*, and from this comes an emphasis on the Arabisation of Islam in non-Arab parts of the Muslim world. The Quran is said to be *tanzil*, i.e. sent down from heaven and therefore a revelation.

Another theme is the example of Muhammad's *hijra*, i.e. migrating to escape from persecution and suffering to achieve a position of political and military power. This brings encouragement that Muslims will eventually triumph.

Tawhid, the unity of Allah, carries with it the concept of bringing all of life into submission under that one God. The awful sin of *shirk* – to associate anything with God – carries the implication that loyalty to the *umma* must transcend any loyalty to a national state. Finally the prohibition of *bida* (innovation) prevents any possibility of adapting Islam for modern times.

Radicals seek to achieve their goal of a worldwide Islamic state (to include the West) by a variety of means. The first stage is to set up an alternative Islamic society in each country that, when strong enough, will take over the state's centres of power. The violent radicals prefer terrorism, revolution and coups as the methods for destabilising states and taking over political power. Others spread Islam to individuals and communities by Muslim mission, *dawa*, often supported by offers of material aid to those who convert. In the West the process is taken forward mainly by seeking to engage with the structures of politics and society so as to carve out space for Islam, as a prelude to Islam's assuming dominance. The demographic effects of large Muslim families and multiple wives look set to have a dramatic impact on societies in many parts of the world within a generation or two, especially in Europe.

PROGRESSIVE (MODERNIST, LIBERAL) ISLAM

Progressives want to reform Islam by Westernising it. They accept the secular separation of religion from the state. They emphasise reason more strongly than revelation. They reinterpret the Quran and *ahadith* in line with secular and liberal, Western concepts of human rights, multiculturalism and equality. They are also willing to use Western academic tools of textual criticism in examining the Muslim scriptures.

Progressives were influential in the 1920s and 1930s and in the early days of independence in the various Muslim states. However, their freedom of expression is now firmly restricted in most Muslim states, where they are under tremendous pressure from Islamists and traditionalists. They face charges of apostasy and blasphemy as well as threats of violence and death; many have therefore emigrated to the West.

Glossary

adhab al-qabr	torments of the grave
adhan	the call to prayer
al-adha	the pilgrims' sacrifice in the valley of *mina* near Mecca
ahl-al-kitab	people of the book (i.e. Jews and Christians)
Ahmadis/Ahmadiyyas	an unorthodox Muslim sect from Pakistan/India, proscribed in some Muslim countries
Allah	the Arabic word for 'God', also used by Arab Christians
amir	commander, leader, prince
arkan-ud-din	the pillars of religion
asr	the afternoon prayer (third prayer time of the day)
ayah	literally 'sign'; verse of the Quran. The Urdu word is *ayat*.
Ayatollah	literally 'sign of Allah'; term of honour for a religious leader in Shia Islam
bani-e-Islam	the founder of Islam, i.e. Muhammad
barzakh	literally an interval, a separation or a partition; the name given to

113

	the intervening state between death and the Last Day
basi bad al-maut	resurrection after death
begum	Urdu word for a respected, married woman
bida	innovation; any doctrine or practice for which no proof exists in the Quran or *sunna*
bismillah	in the name of Allah
burqa	Urdu term for clothing that envelops a woman in public, covering her whole body and face
Caliph	in Arabic *khalifah;* successor, vice-regent, the title used by Sunnis for the supreme spiritual and political leader of the whole Muslim community worldwide (Shias use the word 'imam')
chador	large cloth covering a woman's head and body in public as used in Iran
Dajjal	the Antichrist
Dar al-Harb	literally 'House of War'; classical Islam's term for territory not under Islamic rule
Dar al-Islam	literally 'House of Islam'; territory under Islamic rule
dawa	Islamic mission
dhikr	literally 'remembrance'; the invocation of Allah by repetition of one of his names

dhimmi	non-Muslims in an Islamic society, subjugated people, treated as second-class
din	religion, in its practice
dua	voluntary petitions in prayer
durud	prayer for Muhammad
fajr	dawn; the dawn prayer (first prayer time of the day)
fard	obligatory
fatiha	the first sura of the Quran
fatwa	a published decision concerning religious doctrine or law
fiqh	literally 'understanding'; the science of law, jurisprudence
firman	edict, command, decree
ghusl	bathing the entire body
hadith (pl. *ahadith*)	tradition or report of a precedent set by Muhammad or his early followers
hajj	the annual pilgrimage to Mecca, to be performed by the believer once in a lifetime if economically possible
hajji or hadji	one who has made the pilgrimage to Mecca
hijab	literally 'partition' or 'curtain; the institution of the seclusion of women; often used to mean the woman's head covering that conceals neck, hair and sometimes face

hijra   migration; Muhammad's flight
                                from Mecca to Medina in A.D. 622,
                                which was used as the starting
                                point of the Islamic calendar

Iblis   one of the names of the devil

id-ul-adha   the feast of sacrifice observed
                                seventy days after the end of
                                the fast of Ramadan

id-ul-fitr   the feast that is observed
                                when the fasting month of
                                Ramadan is ended

iftar   the evening meal after each
                                day's fast in Ramadan

ijma   consensus of opinion of the rec-
                                ognised religious authorities at
                                any given time concerning the
                                interpretation and application
                                of the teaching of the Quran in
                                any particular situation

ijtihad   literally 'exertion'; a logical de-
                                duction on a legal or theologi-
                                cal question by a *mujtahid*,
                                as distinguished from *ijma*,
                                which is a collective opinion.
                                Sunnis believe that 'the door
                                of *ijithad* has closed', whereas
                                Shias believe *ijtihad* can still
                                be practised.

imam   leader of a mosque. (In Shia
                                Islam 'imam' is the term used for
                                the leader of the whole Muslim
                                community worldwide.)

iman   faith believed and confessed

Injil	the revelation made by Allah to Jesus; the word occurs ten times in the Quran. Strictly speaking it refers to the Gospels only, but is sometimes applied to the whole New Testament.
isha	the night prayer (the fifth prayer time of the day)
jahiliyya	the state of pagan ignorance and immorality in pre-Islamic Arabian society
janna	literally 'garden'; a term used for paradise
jihad	literally 'striving'. The term has a variety of interpretations including (1) spiritual struggle for moral purity, (2) trying to correct wrong and support right by words and actions, (3) military war in the name of Allah, against non-Muslims with the aim of spreading Islam, against apostates from Islam, or against Muslims with unorthodox theology.
jinn	a spirit, created by Allah. There are some good jinn, but many are evil.
jizya	tax payable by *dhimmi*, as a sign of their subjugation to Muslims

jumma	Friday, the Muslim holy day
Kaaba	cube-shaped shrine at Mecca
kabira	'great' sins
kalima	literally 'word'; Islamic creed
khutba	address (sermon) at Friday mid-day prayers
kismat	it is my lot (an expression of fatalism)
kitab (pl. *kutub*)	book
maghrib	sunset, the evening prayer (fourth prayer time of the day)
Mahdi	literally 'rightly guided one', whose return is awaited by Shia Muslims
majlis	gathering, meeting
maktub	it is written (an expression of fatalism)
malaikah	angels
maqdur	it is decided (an expression of fatalism)
marabout	a religious leader who exercises occult powers. The term is chiefly used in North and West Africa.
mihrab	niche in wall of mosque, indicating direction of prayer (towards Mecca)
miraj	miraculous night-time journey of Muhammad to heaven

mizan	scales on which good and bad deeds are weighed
muezzin	the one who gives out the call to prayer from the mosque
mufti	Sunni scholar, who is an interpreter and expounder of sharia; one who is authorised to issue fatwas
Muharram	the first month of the Islamic year, when the death of Hussain is commemorated from 1st to 10th. Especially observed by Shia Muslims
mujahid (pl. *mujahidin*)	one who goes on jihad; Islamic warrior
mujtahid	literally 'one who strives to obtain a high position and learning'; a very learned religious teacher, one who practices *ijtihad*
mullah	a religious teacher. The term is more common in Pakistan and India.
murshid	see *pir*.
muta	literally 'enjoyment'; a marriage contracted for a limited time, e.g. during a jihad or a pilgrimage; a feature of Shia Islam
nabi	prophet
nikah	marriage, the marriage contract

pir	Persian term for a Sufi holy man, 'saint' or spiritual guide; may also be known as a *murshid* or a sheikh
purdah	literally 'curtain'; the seclusion of women
iqra	read, recite
qibla	direction to which one faces while praying, i.e. towards Mecca
qiyas	analogous reasoning
Quran	the Muslims' holy book
rakah (pl. rakaat)	unit of ritual prayer
Ramadan	the ninth month in the Islamic calendar, the fasting month
Rashidun	the rightly guided ones, used of the first four caliphs following Muhammad
rasul	apostle, messenger, one to whom an inspired book was revealed
riba	some contemporary Muslims consider this to mean 'interest' on money lent, but the traditional meaning was 'extortionate interest'
sadaqa	voluntary offerings made at *id-ul-fitr*
saghira	'little' sins
salah	Muslim ritual prayer recited five times a day
salam	literally 'peace'; a word used as a greeting or salutation

sawm	the act of fasting
shahada	Islamic creed
Sharia	Islamic religious law. *Shariat* is the Urdu word.
Shaytan	one of the names of the devil
sheikh	literally 'old man' or elder. This title can be given to heads of religious orders, Quranic scholars, jurists, those who preach and lead prayers in the mosque, and Sufi saints. It is also used for a village elder or tribal chief.
Shia	the Muslim sect that believes that the rightful successor to Muhammad was Ali, his closest relative
shirk	associating anyone with Allah as a co-deity; the worst sin in Islam
sirat	a very narrow bridge, spanning the fires of hell
Sufi	a mystic
sunna	literally 'a trodden path'; the customs of Muhammad and his early followers who knew him personally
Sunni	literally 'one of the path'; orthodox Islam; the majority, who follow the successors of Muhammad by election

sura
literally 'a row or series'; used exclusively for chapters of the Quran

taifas
small Muslim states in Spain in the 11th, 12th and 13th centuries

takbir
ascription of greatness to Allah

talaq
a word used by a husband to divorce his wife. He must say it three times to her: 'I divorce you, I divorce you, I divorce you.' Then she is considered divorced.

tanzil
literally 'descent'; used to mean revelation; specifically denotes the descent of the Quran from heaven to earth (to Muhammad) via the angel Gabriel

taqdir
the doctrine of predestination

taqiyya
literally 'guarding oneself'; a doctrine by which Shias justify denying some of their religious belief in order to escape persecution; extended to permit lying in a variety of circumstances; also followed by some Sunnis

tasbih
rosary

Taurah
the Torah, the law of Moses, the first five books of the Old Testament, 'taurat' in Urdu

tawaf
circumambulation of the Kaaba seven times

tawhid	unity, oneness; basic doctrine of Islam declaring the absolute oneness of Allah
tayammum	purification by sand or earth (when water is not procurable)
ulama	group of theologians
umma	the whole body of Muslims worldwide
Wahhabis	members of a puritanical reform movement of Sunni Islam founded in the eighteenth century A.D. They are dominant today in Saudi Arabia.
wazir (vizier)	high-ranking political adviser or minister to a Muslim ruler; often the chief minister under the caliph or sultan
wudu/wazu/wuzu	lesser ablution, as distinguished from *ghusl*
yawm al-akhirah	literally 'last day'; day of judgment
Zabur	Psalms
zakat	the alms due from every Muslim
ziyara	a visit to Muhammad's tomb in Medina; has come to mean visits to the tomb of any Muslim saint
zuhr	the mid-day prayer (second prayer time of the day)

APPENDICES

APPENDIX I: A chronology of Muhammad's life

Scholars are unable to pinpoint many of the dates exactly. For example, Muhammad's birth is placed at 20 August 570 by Caussin de Perceval, 20 April 571 by Sprenger and by Mahmud Pasha Falki, and 22 April 571 in the following chronology. The latest research has suggested that most of the facts pertaining to Muhammad's life are shrouded in uncertainty. Muslims would suggest a chronology of Muhammad's life as follows:

Life at MECCA

Birth	12th Rabi al-awwal (Monday, 22 April, A.D. 571) Father, Abdullah, already dead.
Age 6	Death of mother, Aminah
Age 8	Death of grandfather, Abdul Mutalib
Age 12	First business trip to Syria
Age 25	Marriage to Khadijah

Age 40	Beginning of prophethood (A.D. 610)
1st year of prophethood	*Fajr* and *asr* prayers, two *rakaat* each
1st–3rd year	Secret preaching of Islam
At the end of 3rd year	Open call to Islam from Mount Safa, near Mecca
3rd–5th year	Hostility of Meccan infidels
5th year	Migration of Muslims to Abyssinia [Ethiopia]
6th year	Umar accepts Islam
7th–9th year	Continued hostility of Meccan infidels
10th year	Year of Sorrow – deaths of uncle, Abu Talib, and first wife, Khadijah *Miraj* [Muhammad's night journey to heaven], 27th Rajab Five times daily prayers made obligatory during *miraj*
13th year	*Hijrah* to Medina, 27th Safar (A.D 622)

Life at MEDINA

A.H. 1	Arrival at *Quba*, 8th Rabi al-awwal
(first year after the *hijrah*)	Arrival at Medina Establishment of First Islamic State Treaty with the Jews
A.H. 2	Jihad ordained, 12th Safar *Adhan* and *zaka* introduced Revelation about the change of *qibla*, Monday, 15th Shaban Ramadan fast prescribed *Id-ul-fitr*, 1st Shawal Battle of Badr, 17th Ramadan Marriage of Ali and Fatima, after Badr
A.H. 3	First revelation restricting the drinking of wine Battle of Uhud, 5th Shawal First revelation about *riba* (interest) Revelation of laws about orphans, after Uhud Revelation of laws of inheritance Revelation of laws about marriage and the rights of wives
A.H. 4	Revelation of the requirement for *hijab* for women Revelation about the prohibition on drinking wine

A.H. 5	Battle of Dumatul Jandal and battle of Banu al-Mustaliq
	Revelation of laws about adultery and slander
	Battle of Ahzab
A.H. 7	Letters to rulers of different countries including Persian and Roman emperors
	Battle of Khibar
	Revelation of laws about marriage and divorce
A.H. 8	Battle of Mutah
	Conquest of Mecca, 20th Ramadan
	Battle of Hunain
	Siege of Taif
	Revelation of final order prohibiting *riba*
A.H. 9	Battle of Tabuk
	Revelation of order concerning *jizya* tax for non-Muslim minorities
	Hajj prescribed
A.H. 10	Farewell address, 9th Dhul hijjah
A.H. 11	Death, 12th Rabi al-awwal, (A.D. 632)

APPENDIX II: Historical development of Islamic sects

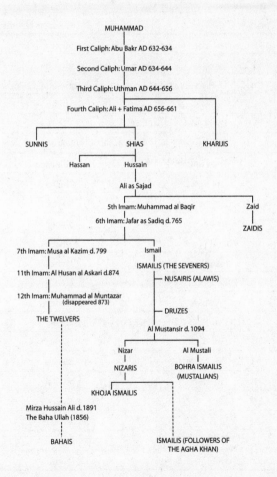

MUHAMMAD

First Caliph: Abu Bakr AD 632-634

Second Caliph: Umar AD 634-644

Third Caliph: Uthman AD 644-656

Fourth Caliph: Ali + Fatima AD 656-661

SUNNIS   SHIAS   KHARIJIS

Hassan   Hussain

Ali as Sajad

5th Imam: Muhammad al Baqir   Zaid

6th Imam: Jafar as Sadiq d. 765   ZAIDIS

7th Imam: Musa al Kazim d. 799   Ismail

11th Imam: Al Husan al Askari d. 874   ISMAILIS (THE SEVENERS)

12th Imam: Muhammad al Muntazar   NUSAIRIS (ALAWIS)
(disappeared 873)

THE TWELVERS   DRUZES

                              Al Mustansir d. 1094

                    Nizar   Al Mustali

                    NIZARIS   BOHRA ISMAILIS
                                       (MUSTALIANS)

                KHOJA ISMAILIS

Mirza Hussain Ali d. 1891
The Baha Ullah (1856)

BAHAIS   ISMAILIS (FOLLOWERS OF
                                THE AGHA KHAN)

Appendix III: Suras of the Quran

There are 114 suras (chapters), of which 88 are Meccan and 26 Medinan.

Sura Number	Sura Name	Revealed in Mecca or Medina
1	The Exordium (Introduction)	Mecca
2	The Cow	Medina
3	The Family of Imran	Medina
4	The Woman	Medina
5	The Table	Medina
6	The Cattle	Mecca
7	The Heights	Mecca
8	The Spoils	Medina
9	The Repentance	Medina
10	Jonah	Mecca
11	Hud	Mecca
12	Joseph	Mecca
13	Thunder	Medina
14	Abraham	Mecca
15	The Rocky Tract [Hijr]	Mecca
16	The Bee	Mecca
17	The Night Journey	Mecca
18	The Cave	Mecca
19	Mary	Mecca
20	Ta Ha	Mecca
21	The Prophets	Mecca
22	The Pilgrimage	Medina

23	The Believers	Mecca
24	Light	Medina
25	The Criteron	Mecca
26	The Poets	Mecca
27	The Ants	Mecca
28	Narration	Mecca
29	The Spider	Mecca
30	The Romans	Mecca
31	Luqman	Mecca
32	Adoration	Mecca
33	The Confederates	Medina
34	Saba	Mecca
35	The Creator	Mecca
36	Ya Sin	Mecca
37	The Ranks	Mecca
38	Sad	Mecca
39	The Crowds	Mecca
40	The Believer	Mecca
41	Fussilat	Mecca
42	Consultation	Mecca
43	Gold Ornaments	Mecca
44	Smoke	Mecca
45	Kneeling	Mecca
46	Sand Tracts [Ajqaf]	Mecca
47	Muhammad	Medina
48	Victory	Medina
49	The Chambers	Medina

50	Oaf	Mecca
51	The Winds	Mecca
52	The Mountain	Mecca
53	The Star	Mecca
54	The Moon	Mecca
55	Merciful	Mecca
56	The Inevitable Event	Mecca
57	The Iron	Medina
58	She who pleaded	Medina
59	The Banishment	Medina
60	She who is tested	Medina
61	The Battle Array	Medina
62	Friday	Medina
63	The Hypocrites	Medina
64	Cheating	Medina
65	Divorce	Medina
66	The Prohibition	Medina
67	Dominion	Mecca
68	The Pen	Medina
69	The Sure Reality	Mecca
70	The Ways of Ascent	Mecca
71	Noah	Mecca
72	The Jinns	Mecca
73	The Mantled One	Mecca
74	The Cloaked One	Mecca
75	The Resurrection	Mecca
76	Man	Mecca

77	Those sent forth	Mecca
78	Tidings	Mecca
79	The Soul-Snatchers	Mecca
80	He Frowned	Mecca
81	The Folding Up	Mecca
82	The Cataclysm	Mecca
83	The Just	Mecca
84	The Rending Asunder	Mecca
85	The Constellation	Mecca
86	The Night Visitor	Mecca
87	The Most High	Mecca
88	The Overwhelming Event	Mecca
89	The Break of Day	Mecca
90	The City	Mecca
91	The Sun	Mecca
92	The Night	Mecca
93	Daylight	Mecca
94	The Expansion	Mecca
95	The Fig	Mecca
96	The Blood Clot	Mecca
97	The Night of Power	Mecca
98	The Clear Evidence	Mecca
99	The Convulsion	Mecca
100	The War Steeds	Mecca
101	The Day of Noise and Clamour	Mecca
102	Piling Up	Mecca
103	The Declining Day	Mecca

104	The Scandal-Monger	Mecca
105	The Elephant	Mecca
106	The Quraysh	Mecca
107	Alms	Mecca
108	Abundance	Mecca
109	The Unbelievers	Mecca
110	Help	Medina
111	Lahab	Mecca
112	Purity of Faith	Mecca
113	The Dawn	Mecca
114	Mankind	Mecca

Bibliography

Adeney, M. *Daughters of Islam: Building Bridges with Muslim Women*. Downers Grove, IL, IVP, 2002

Al-Hilali, Muhammad Taqi-ud-Din and Khan, Muhammad Muhsin. *Interpretation of the Meanings of the Noble Quran in the English Language: A summarised version of At-Tabari, Al-Qurtabi and Ibn Kathir with comments from Sahih Al-Bukhari*. Fifteenth revised edition, Riyadh, Darussalam Publishers and Distributors, 1996

Ali, Abdullah Yusuf. *The Meaning of the Holy Quran*. New edition with revised translation and commentary, Beltsville, Maryland, Amana Publications, 1995

Ali, Ameer. *The Spirit of Islam: a Shi'ite view of Islam*. London, Oxford University Press, 1967

Arberry, A.J. *Sufism: an account of the mystics of Islam*. London, George Allen & Unwin, 1979

Beck, Lois and Keddie, Nikki (editors). *Women in the Muslim World*. London, Harvard University Press, 1978

Braswell, G. *What You Need to Know About Islam & Muslims*. Nashville, Broadman & Holman, 2000

Cook, Michael. *The Koran: A Very Short Introduction*. Oxford, Oxford University Press, 2000

Cook, Michael. *Muhammad*. Oxford, Oxford University Press, 1983

Geisler, N L & Saleeb, A. *Answering Islam*. Grand Rapids, MI, Baker Books, 1993

Gilchrist, John. *Is Muhammad Foretold in the Bible?* Sheffield, FFM Publications, 1979

Gilchrist, John. *Origins and Sources of the Gospel of Barnabas*. Sheffield, FFM Publications, 1979

Gospel of Barnabas. Translated by Lonsdale and Laura Ragg. Oxford, Clarendon Press, 1907

Hughes, Thomas Patrick. *A Dictionary of Islam*. Lahore, Kazi Publications, modern reprint of 1885 edition

Iliff, Frances P. *Salam Alekum: Understanding Muslim culture to make friends*. London, Interserve, 1995

Jeffery, Patricia. *Frogs in a Well: Indian women in Purdah*. London, Zed Press, 1979

Nicholson, R.A. *The Mystics of Islam: Sufism*. London, Routledge & Kegan Paul, 1979

Riddell, Peter G. and Peter Cotterell. *Islam in Context: Past, Present, and Future*. Grand Rapids, MI, Baker Books, 2003

Rippin, Andrew. *Muslims: Their Religious Beliefs and Practices: The Formative Period*. London & New York, Routledge, 1990

Ruthven, Malise. *Islam in the World*. Oxford, Oxford University Press, 2000

Sookhdeo, Patrick. *Faith, Power and Territory: A Handbook of British Islam*. McLean, VA, Isaac Publishing, 2008

Sookhdeo, Patrick. *The Challenge of Islam to the Church and Its Mission*. McLean, VA, Isaac Publishing, 2008

Sookhdeo, Patrick. *Understanding Shari'a Finance: The Muslim Challenge to Western Economics*. McLean, VA, Isaac Publishing, 2008

Sookhdeo, Rosemary. *Secrets Behind the Burqa*. McLean, VA, Isaac Publishing, 2004

Sookhdeo, Rosemary. *Stepping Into the Shadows: Why Women Convert to Islam*. Pewsey, Isaac Publishing, 2007

Steer, Malcolm. *An Evangelistic Christian's Pocket Guide to Islam*. Fearn, Christian Focus Publications, 2008

Zeidan, David. *Sword of Allah*. Waynesboro, GA, Gabriel Publishing, 2003

A Christian's
Pocket Guide to

Buddhism

Alex Smith

A Christian's Pocket Guide to Buddhism

ALEX G. SMITH

Published in conjunction with OMF. Buddhism has existed for over 2,500 years. Like Christianity it has faced persecution. While it started as mainly an Asian religion it is now beginning to have considerable growth in the west and is the fastest growing religion in Australia and has some two thousand temples in the USA.

If you compare Christianity and Buddhism you will see many contrasts. For example, a Buddhist would not believe in a supreme God who created the universe or in fact anything supernatural. They believe in 'making merit'. Christianity talks about communicating the gospel of a loving God who gives mercy, hope and an exchanged life.

This guide will help you overcome the hurdles and communicate the gospel in a way that Buddhists can understand. So whether you are travelling, or meet a Buddhist in your workplace or next door, this book will be an invaluable tool in this cross-cultural age.

OMF (Overseas Missionary Fellowship) are specialists in Christian interaction with people from Asia.

ISBN 978-7-84550-526-4

A Christian's Pocket Guide to

the Japanese

A Christian's
Pocket Guide to
the Japanese

OMF INTERNATIONAL

Globalisation means that increasingly we meet people
from a wider variety of nations and cultures.

The manufacturing revolution that has seen Japan
become one of the top industrialised nations in the world
means that more Japanese people are travelling abroad
and more people are travelling to Japan.

What should Christian's know about the Japanese?
That question is answered by this book.

A Christian's Pocket Guide to the Japanese firstly
looks at the history, culture and religions common in Japan - and their attitude to Christianity.

Secondly, it gives guidance on how to befriend Japanese people (including a life-saving 'Do's' and 'Don'ts'
section) and thirdly how best to talk to them about Christianity itself.

There are also useful appendices with suggested further reading and how to lead a Bible study.

If you meet people from Japan at work, school or
socially - or if you travel to Japan - then this is an
invaluable book.

OMF (Overseas Missionary Fellowship) are specialists
in Christian interaction with people from Asia.

ISBN 978-7-84550-316-1

The organisations which contributed to this book

FELLOWSHIP OF FAITH FOR THE MUSLIMS
P.O. Box 5864, Basildon SS13 3FF, UK
E-mail: admin@f-f-m.org.uk

The Fellowship of Faith for the Muslims (FFM) is a prayer fellowship that seeks to encourage Christians to pray for the Muslim world and so to this end publishes a regular prayer bulletin.

INSTITUTE FOR THE STUDY OF ISLAM AND CHRISTIANITY
9 & 10, Priory Row, Coventry CV1 5EX, UK

A Christian research institute focusing on the status of the Church in the Muslim world and current trends in Islam. It is also involved in training and the dissemination of information.

BARNABAS FUND
The Old Rectory, River Street, Pewsey, Wiltshire, SN9 5DB, UK
E-mail: info@barnabasfund.org

A charity supporting the suffering Church, particularly in the Muslim world, by prayer and funding for small-scale projects which help specifically Christians.

Christian Focus Publications

publishes books for all ages

Our mission statement –

STAYING FAITHFUL

In dependence upon God we seek to impact the world through literature faithful to His infallible Word, the Bible. Our aim is to ensure that the LORD Jesus Christ is presented as the only hope to obtain forgiveness of sin, live a useful life and look forward to heaven with Him.

REACHING OUT

Christ's last command requires us to reach out to our world with His gospel. We seek to help fulfil that by publishing books that point people towards Jesus and help them develop a Christ-like maturity. We aim to equip all levels of readers for life, work, ministry and mission.

Books in our adult range are published in three imprints.

Christian Focus contains popular works including biographies, commentaries, basic doctrine and Christian living. Our children's books are also published in this imprint.

Mentor focuses on books written at a level suitable for Bible College and seminary students, pastors, and other serious readers. The imprint includes commentaries, doctrinal studies, examination of current issues and church history.

Christian Heritage contains classic writings from the past.

Christian Focus Publications Ltd,
Geanies House, Fearn, Ross-shire,
IV20 1TW, Scotland, United Kingdom
info@christianfocus.com
www.christianfocus.com